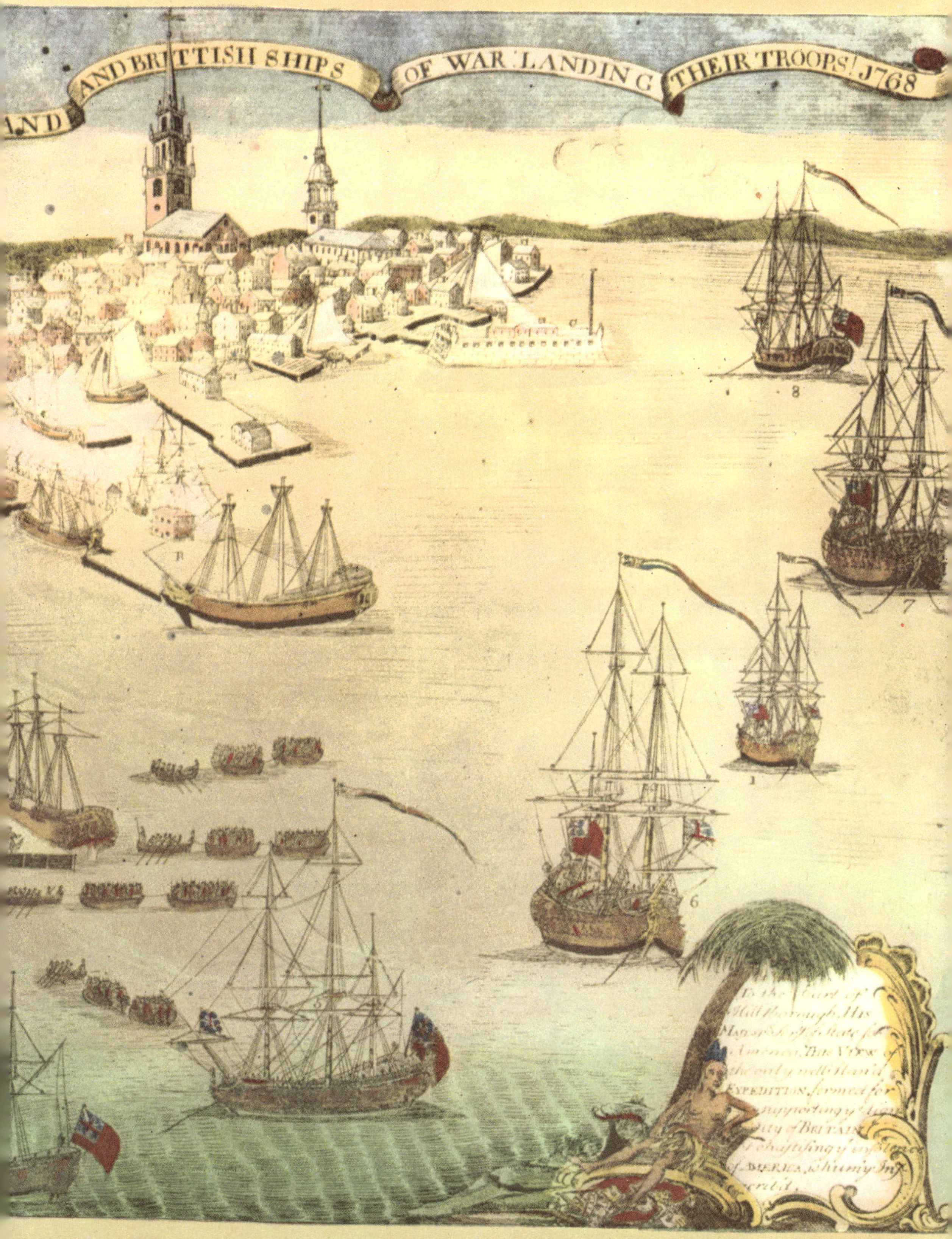

LEXINGTON, CONCORD AND BUNKER HILL

BY THE EDITORS OF
AMERICAN HERITAGE
The Magazine of History

AUTHOR
FRANCIS RUSSELL

CONSULTANT
RICHARD M. KETCHUM
Author of THE BATTLE FOR BUNKER HILL

PUBLISHED BY
AMERICAN HERITAGE PUBLISHING CO., INC., NEW YORK

FIRST EDITION

© 1963 by American Heritage Publishing Co., Inc., 551 Fifth Avenue, New York 17, New York. All rights reserved under Berne and Pan-American Copyright Conventions. U.S. Copyright disclaimed for color plates except those on pages 29 and 40. Library of Congress Catalog Card Number: 63-10834.

BOOK TRADE DISTRIBUTION BY MEREDITH PRESS

INSTITUTIONAL DISTRIBUTION BY HARPER & ROW

Mounted couriers spread the fateful news of the clash on Lexington Common to aroused minutemen in William T. Ranney's nineteenth-century painting.

Foreword

The opening scenes in the stirring drama of the American Revolution were acted out nearly two centuries ago. The leading actors and events —John Hancock and Samuel Adams; the Boston Tea Party, Lexington and Concord, Bunker Hill—have assumed a cherished place in our history. Yet, with the passage of time, a layer of legend and romance has settled over these scenes, sometimes obscuring the true picture.

The legend persists that the Revolution was brought about by moderate men rebelling against harsh British tyranny. As Francis Russell points out in this book, however, the cause of liberty was spearheaded by radical leaders whose strident cries drowned out the voices of the moderates. Both the Boston Massacre and the Boston Tea Party, for example, were the result of mob violence sparked by such men as Adams and Hancock. We sometimes forget that in the decade before the Revolution Boston and other American cities were at times ruled by brutal street mobs that sacked the homes of officials and assaulted anyone who dared oppose them.

A haze of romance also shrouds the first battles of the war. The minutemen who fought the redcoats on April 19, 1775, were not quite the deadly marksmen later generations have supposed—only one of every three hundred bullets they fired hit anything. And for every colonial who faced with cool courage the British bayonets at Bunker Hill, two others fled at the first shots or refused to aid their hard-pressed comrades. This first major engagement of the war is even misnamed. It was not fought on Bunker Hill at all, but on nearby Breed's Hill.

What this proves, of course, is that the Americans who made the Revolution were only human beings, not supermen. They were challenging the greatest military power of their time, and if they were sometimes badly led or made mistakes or ran from the sound of the guns, it is not to be wondered at. It should be a special source of pride to realize that enough of these ordinary, everyday people stood up to the dreaded redcoats at Lexington and Concord and Breed's Hill to finally triumph.

This book presents, whenever possible, paintings, sketches, and engravings by men who were actually there. Here are the faces of patriot leaders and English generals by such painters as Copley and Stuart; detailed views of the Breed's Hill fighting by British officers; engravings of Lexington and Concord, done crudely but with the accuracy of firsthand observation.

Some of these pictures, in fact, played a part in bringing about the Revolution. Paul Revere's view of the Boston Massacre was a potent piece of propaganda that was selling widely—and cheaply—within three weeks after the riot. Such pictorial representations of the critical events of the day dramatized the widening gulf between colonies and mother country and helped to turn public opinion against England and her policies.

The Revolution was to last six long and bloody years before the thirteen colonies won their independence, yet the pattern was set in those first few months. Against long odds, and despite military defeat, the Americans hung on grimly and won their objective. Fortunately, they were willing to accept Patrick Henry's grim terms: "I know not what course others may take; but for me, give me liberty or give me death!"

—The Editors

Six new AMERICAN HERITAGE JUNIOR LIBRARY *books are published each year. Titles currently available are:*

LEXINGTON, CONCORD AND BUNKER HILL	THE CALIFORNIA GOLD RUSH
CLIPPER SHIPS AND CAPTAINS	PIRATES OF THE SPANISH MAIN
D-DAY, THE INVASION OF EUROPE	TRAPPERS AND MOUNTAIN MEN
WESTWARD ON THE OREGON TRAIL	MEN OF SCIENCE AND INVENTION
THE FRENCH AND INDIAN WARS	NAVAL BATTLES AND HEROES
GREAT DAYS OF THE CIRCUS	THOMAS JEFFERSON AND HIS WORLD
STEAMBOATS ON THE MISSISSIPPI	DISCOVERERS OF THE NEW WORLD
COWBOYS AND CATTLE COUNTRY	RAILROADS IN THE DAYS OF STEAM
TEXAS AND THE WAR WITH MEXICO	INDIANS OF THE PLAINS
THE PILGRIMS AND PLYMOUTH COLONY	THE STORY OF YANKEE WHALING

American Heritage also publishes HORIZON CARAVEL BOOKS, *a similar series on world history, culture, and the arts. Titles currently available are:*

NELSON AND THE AGE OF FIGHTING SAIL
ALEXANDER THE GREAT   HEROES OF POLAR EXPLORATION
RUSSIA UNDER THE CZARS   KNIGHTS OF THE CRUSADES

COVER: *Archibald Willard's famous 1876 canvas captures the spirit of the colonists in the critical first year of the Revolution.*
ABBOT HALL, MARBLEHEAD

FRONT ENDSHEET: *Paul Revere engraved this scene of British regiments landing at Boston's Long Wharf in the autumn of 1768.*
COLLECTION OF VALENTINE HOLLINGSWORTH, JR.

BACK ENDSHEET: *John Trumbull's painting of the death of Joseph Warren at Bunker Hill is romantic historical art at its best.*
YALE UNIVERSITY ART GALLERY

Contents

1	Shots Heard Round the World	10
2	Rising of the Wind	38
3	The Redcoats Challenged	70
4	Bunker Hill	94
5	Boston Besieged	126
	Acknowledgments	148
	For Further Reading	149
	Index	150

ILLUSTRATED WITH PAINTINGS, DRAWINGS, MAPS, AND ENGRAVINGS, MANY OF THE PERIOD

1

Shots Heard Round the World

"I then went Home, took my Boots and Surtout, and went to the North part of the Town, Where I had kept a Boat; two friends rowed me across Charles River, a little to the eastward where the Somerset Man of War lay. It was then young flood, the Ship was winding, and the moon was Rising. They landed me on Charlestown side ... and I went to git me a Horse."

So wrote Paul Revere in his account of his ride of April 18, 1775, the most famous ride in American history. He and his two friends were lucky to slip across the river so easily, for the *Somerset,* with sentinels alert, was anchored in the channel to prevent just such a crossing—and the moon was full that night. But they managed to muffle their oars with a petticoat they had borrowed on the way from a friendly young lady, and reached the opposite shore unobserved.

Boston, behind them, was a virtual garrison town, with 4,000 British troops quartered among the 20,000 inhabitants. Ever since June, 1774—six months after Bostonians masquerading as Indians had dumped the East India Company's tea into the harbor—the port of Boston had been closed by act of Parliament. Closed it would remain, His Majesty's government announced, until the tea was paid for.

The force to padlock the Boston peninsula was furnished by nine regiments of regulars, plus parts of two others. Many of these troops had disembarked in the spring of 1774. From Ireland had come the King's Own, the 5th, the 38th, the 43rd, and three companies of the Royal Irish. The Royal Welch Fusiliers and their goat mascot arrived from New York. Be-

Paul Revere was an engraver and master silversmith as well as a courier for the Massachusetts political radicals. Holding a teapot of his own design, Revere was painted about 1765 by his friend John Singleton Copley.

sides the numbered regiments, there were enough marines to make up a regiment of their own, and an artillery train that camped on Boston Common.

While Boston's commercial life withered, affairs were humming in the outlying, unoccupied towns. Growing numbers of Whigs, as they called themselves—those who in varying degrees and for varying reasons were opposed to the royal authority—had been gathering together stores of powder and supplies for a foreseeable clash with the redcoats. On village greens across New England the "minutemen" had begun to drill, preparing for action at a minute's notice.

Military security was not a part of the eighteenth-century consciousness, and talk and information flowed freely in and out of Boston. Lieutenant General the Honorable Thomas Gage, governor of the Province of Massachusetts Bay and commander of all His Majesty's forces in the American colonies, knew where nearly all of the colonists' ammunition dumps were hidden. The colonists in turn were aware of every British troop movement almost as soon as General Gage had issued his orders.

By the fifteenth of April, 1775, it was clear that the redcoats were up to something. Boats belonging to the troop transports were being tested, and grenadiers and light infantry were taken off duty and assembled on the common.

Two of the most outspoken Whigs, Samuel Adams and John Hancock, had wisely left Boston and were staying in Lexington. They planned to leave soon for Philadelphia as delegates to the Second Continental Congress. The First Continental Congress, that assembly of twelve of the thirteen colonies that met the year before, had respectfully set forth American grievances to King George III, but had made no claim to independence. Sam Adams undoubtedly hoped for more violent things from the Second.

Paul Revere, skilled silversmith and well-known Boston citizen, had often served as a trusted messenger for the Whigs, carrying their most secret dispatches to New York and Philadelphia. On Sunday, April 16, he was sent to Lexington by the amiable and tireless Dr. Joseph Warren to warn Adams and Hancock that Gage's troops were planning a sortie—a sortie probably aimed at seizing them as well as the large ammunition dump at nearby Concord.

Revere rode to Lexington and back, without haste and without incident. Returning by way of Charlestown, he dropped in on the local militia colonel, William Conant, to tell him that he would try to reach Charlestown when the British moved. In case he could not get across the river he would arrange to show a signal light from the steeple of the North Church—two lanterns if they left by boats, one if they started overland.

Two days later, Tuesday, April 18, General Gage had completed his arrangements. Each British regiment was made up of eight companies of foot soldiers, a company of light infantry, and one of grenadiers. The light infantry and grenadiers were picked troops—the light infantry chosen for their dash and boldness as skirmishers, the grenadiers for their height and strength. Some seven hundred of these troops, under the command of Lieutenant Colonel Francis Smith, were to embark from the foot of the common, cross over to Cambridge, and march through Menotomy (Arlington) and Lexington seventeen miles to Concord.

There they would seize and destroy all "Artillery, Ammunition, Provisions, Tents, Small Arms, and all Military Stores whatever." General Gage doubted that "the damned rebels would take up arms against his Majesty's Troops." Smith's second-in-command was Major John Pitcairn of the Royal Marines, a bluff soldier who had been billeted almost next door to the Reveres and who was well-liked even by those Bostonians who disliked the British most.

By Tuesday afternoon Colonel Smith's men were in battle order, and it was clear that they were ready to march. But where? The answer was soon furnished Revere and his friends by a groom who had overheard some of the younger officers joking in the stables. Concord was their goal!

At nightfall the boats were drawn up just beyond the common, and the redcoats prepared to embark. Before slipping away on his chancy venture, Revere told the young sexton of the North Church, Robert Newman, to flash the double signal. If Revere did not get through with his message, the signal would. As added insurance, a rotund young shoemaker named William Dawes set out on the land route in an attempt to carry the message past the British lines on Boston Neck.

After Revere had rowed across the Charles, he found Colonel Conant and a group of friends waiting in Charlestown to learn "what was Acting." The colonel said he had seen the signal lights and added that groups of British officers were already patrolling the roads leading to Cambridge and Concord. Revere borrowed "a very good Horse" from Deacon John Larkin and set out for Lexington, twelve miles away.

The colonists relied upon post riders, like the one in this old woodcut, for letters and the latest news of relations with England.

This flag, proclaiming boldly in Latin "Conquer or Die," was carried by the Bedford minutemen in the fighting at Concord's North Bridge.

Adept smuggler and master of disguise, thirty-year-old William Dawes (right) slipped by the British patrols at Boston Neck to spread the alarm.

Charlestown was then, like Boston, an oval promontory attached to the mainland by a stemlike neck. At about 11 P.M. Revere rode over the neck at a slow canter, the Mystic River on his right, the Charles on his left. So bright was the moon that it cast shadows.

Across the neck the road forked—left to Cambridge, right to Medford. Turning left, he began to cross a flat, barren marshland known as Charlestown Common. Years before, a slave named Mark had been executed for murdering his master, and his body had been left hanging in an iron cage as a warning. As Revere passed the rusted cage with its heap of bones, he caught a glimpse of two British officers waiting on horseback under a tree, their holsters and cockades outlined in the moonlight. One of them spurred toward him while the other stayed behind and blocked the road.

Revere turned sharply and galloped back. The officer trying to cut him off became bogged down in a mudhole. "I got clear of him," Revere wrote, "and went thro Medford, over the Bridge, and up to Menotomy. In Medford, I awaked the Captain of the Minute men; and after that, I alarmed almost every House, till I got to Lexington."

Once at Lexington he went to Reverend Jonas Clark's house to warn Adams and Hancock that the troops were on the way. He had been there about half an hour when William Dawes turned up, none the worse for wear. The two messengers did not seem to be in a great hurry, for before they set out for Concord they "refreshid" themselves. Along the way they were overtaken by young Dr.

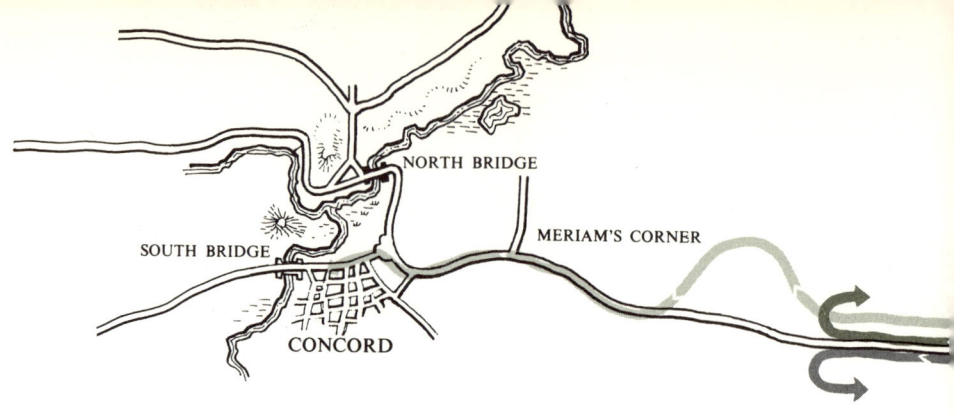

Samuel Prescott of Concord, returning from courting a lady friend in Lexington. Prescott asked to go along. At each house the three came to, they roused the inhabitants.

Halfway to Concord they were stopped by another British patrol. "In an instant I saw four of them," Revere recalled, "who rode up to me, with thier pistols in their hands, said G–d d–n you stop. If you go an Inch further, you are a dead Man; immeaditly Mr. Prescot came up we attempted to git thro them, but they kept before us, and swore if we did not turn in to that pasture, they would blow our brains out."

Turn in they did. Prescott managed to jump his horse over a low stone wall and got away to Concord. Dawes made a dash for it and got to a nearby farmhouse, where he fell off his horse and lost his watch. He then escaped on foot.

Revere headed for a wood at the far end of the pasture and was at once seized and hauled from his horse by six officers concealed there. The major in command—much of a gentleman, according to Revere—questioned him. With the indifference of the times to matters that would later be considered top secret, Revere said that he had left Boston at ten o'clock and that he had been alerting the countryside ever since.

The British patrol had already picked up four other prisoners and these, with Revere, were taken back along the road toward Lexington. Some of the young officers, less gentlemanly than the major, jeered at their prisoners, and one of them told Revere he was in a "d–m–d critical situation." Revere replied that he was "sensible of it."

After about a mile the other prisoners were ordered to dismount, saddles and bridles were cut from their horses, and the animals driven away. The men were then allowed to go free. Revere had been handed over to a sergeant who had orders to shoot him if he tried to escape. The sergeant now decided he preferred Revere's horse to his own. Revere could hardly object. The major asked him a few more questions; then he too was allowed to go free—on foot.

So the swift night rider of poem and legend actually ended his journey, not with a clatter of hurrying hoofs, but plodding horseless across fields and through the Lexington burying ground

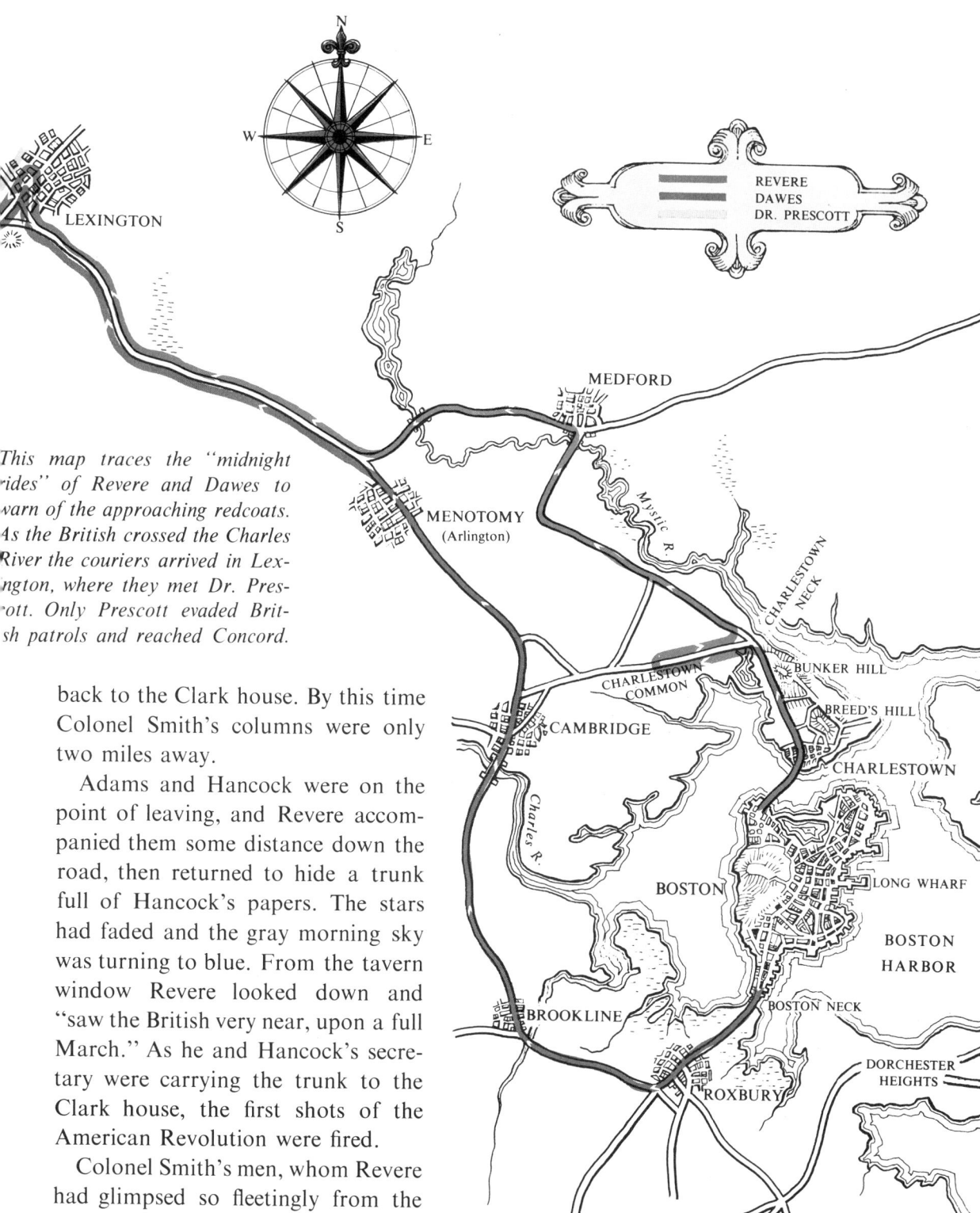

This map traces the "midnight rides" of Revere and Dawes to warn of the approaching redcoats. As the British crossed the Charles River the couriers arrived in Lexington, where they met Dr. Prescott. Only Prescott evaded British patrols and reached Concord.

back to the Clark house. By this time Colonel Smith's columns were only two miles away.

Adams and Hancock were on the point of leaving, and Revere accompanied them some distance down the road, then returned to hide a trunk full of Hancock's papers. The stars had faded and the gray morning sky was turning to blue. From the tavern window Revere looked down and "saw the British very near, upon a full March." As he and Hancock's secretary were carrying the trunk to the Clark house, the first shots of the American Revolution were fired.

Colonel Smith's men, whom Revere had glimpsed so fleetingly from the tavern window, had had a rough night of it. At 10 P.M. they had assembled at the foot of Boston Common in

Our knowledge of the conflicts of April 19 owes much to the crude but accurate engravings of minuteman Amos Doolittle, who based them on paintings by a fellow soldier, Ralph Earle. The redcoats are shown opening fire at the dispersing Lexington minutemen. The officer on horseback is Major Pitcairn.

marching order, waiting to be ferried over to the Cambridge shore. Then, in a manner common to armies before and since, nothing happened. Everyone was ready to move except Colonel Smith, a plump, overage, and fussily inefficient commander. By the time Smith gave the order to embark, it was after eleven, and it was after midnight before the last detachments were landed.

Then, for two more hours, the troops squatted on the mudbanks while the tide rose around them. Disgustedly they chewed on their field rations, then threw away what was left. Not until after 2 A.M. did they finally take the road for Lexington and Concord, marching in surly columns under the white moonlight, wet to the waist and no doubt cursing the day they ever came to America. There were ten companies of light infantry and eleven of grenadiers in that line of march. It had taken them four hours to go their first half mile.

In the pale morning light they neared Lexington Common, the light infantry in front, the grenadiers in the rear. Suddenly they heard the roll of a drum beating the call to arms, sharp and threatening, rapped out by sixteen-year-old William Diamond. At the sound Major Pitcairn, commanding the advance on horseback, halted the redcoats and gave them orders to prime and load. Then, after doubling in ranks, they advanced again at double-quick time.

Strung across the green triangle of the common, on the other side of the white meetinghouse, waited a straggling line of thirty-eight minutemen commanded by Captain John Parker.

Parker, forty-five years old, had served with Rogers' Rangers in the French Wars, and there were others in his little group who had once fought side by side with the redcoats. Old Robert Munroe was a hero at the siege of Louisbourg thirty years before. To the apprehensive villagers at the far end of the common, the line of minutemen must have seemed fearfully thin. Captain Parker, no fool, ordered his men to give ground to the regulars, to disperse, and above all not to fire.

Why the captain had led his men to such a hopelessly exposed position is still mystifying, but it may well be that he was persuaded by Samuel Adams. Adams may have felt—probably did feel—that once the minutemen and the redcoats came face to face bloodshed would be inevitable, and he counted on the shock of such an encounter to unify the colonies against the mother country.

General Gage had given emphatic orders not to molest the inhabitants. Gage, an easygoing man with an American wife, wanted no trouble with the New Englanders, who were to him first of all subjects—if erring subjects—of His Majesty. Mindful of this, and sharing the same feelings, Major Pitcairn shouted to his advancing light infantry, "Soldiers, don't fire! Keep your ranks! Surround and

disarm them!" His voice rang out even as Captain Parker was ordering his minutemen not to fire.

The infantry moved to the right of the meetinghouse, Pitcairn and his junior officers galloping to the left. After a night of waiting and marching, the redcoats—hungry, damp, and chilled, their pipe-clayed gaiters and breeches sodden with mud—were in a black mood. As they gripped their muskets and trotted at the double-quick, they began the hoarse familiar shout of the advancing British battle line. The minutemen began to break up and saunter away.

Suddenly a shot echoed across Lexington Common. Just who fired it, whether colonial or regular, whether deliberately or by accident, would never be known. But at its sound the angry and now disorderly line of redcoats began to fire at will. Furiously Major Pitcairn turned on his soldiers, spurring his horse into the ranks, his sword flashing downward in the signal of cease-fire. But the men, in their aroused battle anger, paid no heed.

The fateful engagements at Lexington and Concord are recorded in this 1775 English picture-map. The first colonial dead lie on Lexington Common (upper left). Nearby, at Concord's North Bridge, minutemen dressed in blue exact their revenge. The British retreat to Boston is harassed by companies of provincials as other minutemen (top, mistakenly colored in red) swarm in from outlying towns. Also shown are the American camps that soon ringed Boston.

21

Hard-driving Major John Pitcairn was one of the most able and popular British officers. Two months after the Lexington disaster, he was mortally wounded at Breed's Hill.
LEXINGTON HISTORICAL SOCIETY

About eight minutemen managed a return fire against the haphazard volleys.

Smoke swirled across the spring grass, blurring the figures of the disappearing minutemen, outlining the redcoats who continued firing in spite of their officers' bellowed commands. Into the confusion—late again—rode Colonel Smith. At once he ordered the drummer to beat assembly, and at the staccato ruffle the soldiers at last held their fire.

Eight of Captain Parker's makeshift company, among them Robert Munroe, lay dead in the new grass. Nine others were wounded. They were—as Samuel Adams at once sensed—the first casualties of the American Revolution.

Under Colonel Smith's hard eye and lashing tongue the light infantry again formed ranks. As they marched past the deserted common, they fired a victory volley and gave the traditional three cheers for a successful engagement.

The sun was well above the treetops in a cloudless sky as the scarlet columns took the straight, six-mile road to Concord. Warmed by the sun and by the excitement of the skirmish, with drums beating and fifes shrilling, the troops marched in renewed good spirits. It would be an easy jaunt to Concord to seize the stores, they thought, and the end of the afternoon would see them easily back in Boston.

With the first night-warning of the advance of the regulars, lame, elderly Colonel James Barrett, commanding the Concord militia, began assembling his minutemen; he also sent out messengers to summon detachments from neighboring communities. By the time the news came through that there had been firing at Lexington, 250 minutemen had gathered in Concord. As soon as he heard it, Major John Buttrick formed them into four companies and marched them down the Lexington road behind their own fife and drum corps.

They had gone a mile and a half when they heard the squeal of approaching fifes and glimpsed the scarlet advance column. Major Buttrick halted his little force until the redcoats were less than two hundred yards away, then turned his men about and marched them back toward

Concord. Minutemen and redcoats kept their marching distance on the same road; there were no challenges, no shots, only the thump and whistle of the two sets of fifers and drummers. "We had a grand musick," minuteman Amos Barrett wrote afterward.

About a mile from the village, the minutemen left the highway and climbed the sandy ridge paralleling the road. Colonel Smith sent detachments of light infantry as flankers to follow them along the ridge while he continued with the main body toward Concord. The redcoats reached the center of the village at eight o'clock, halting on the common opposite Wright's Tavern.

Meanwhile, the minutemen had paused near the meetinghouse and their liberty pole, but as the light infantry flankers approached they moved to a safer slope beyond the burying ground. Groups of volunteers steadily trickled in from the outlying villages—Carlisle, Bedford, Acton.

Colonel Barrett, out of reach but not out of sight of the British, held a council of war with his lieutenants. After some debate they prudently decided to retreat over the North Bridge to the far side of the Concord River. There, on a hillock a few hundred yards from the bridge, the minutemen could wait for more volunteers and still see and hear what was going on in the village.

Colonel Smith knew that when he got back to Boston there would undoubtedly be a court of inquiry about the Lexington skirmish, and he was determined that nothing of the kind was going to be repeated in Concord. The morning seemed placid, the village calm. Smith and Major Pitcairn climbed up to the burying ground and stood among the slate tombstones, the colonel studying his maps while the major inspected the landscape through a spyglass.

On his return to the common, Smith sent Captain Parsons and the troublesome light infantry outside the village limits, one company to guard South Bridge over the Concord River, seven others to follow after the minutemen retreating over the North Bridge. His grenadiers—his best soldiers, all of them at least six feet tall—remained in Concord where they conducted a most genteel door-to-door search, scrupulously observing their colonel's orders not to molest private property.

The only property they damaged was the jail. Ephraim Jones, jailkeeper and innkeeper, had bolted all the doors. When the grenadiers, on Pitcairn's order, finally broke in, they found three cannon hidden inside. Nevertheless, jailkeeper Jones was released so that innkeeper Jones could prepare the major's breakfast.

At Ebenezer Hubbard's malthouse the soldiers found a number of barrels

OVERLEAF: *Steady ranks of British regulars march into Concord as Major Pitcairn (with spyglass) and Colonel Smith observe the situation. This is the only surviving Earle painting of the events at Lexington and Concord.*
COLLECTION OF MRS. STEDMAN BUTTRICK

of flour, which they began to smash; then, to save themselves the trouble, they threw barrels and all into the millpond. While the redcoats were going about dismantling cannon, tossing flour, cannon balls, and lead shot into the water, and foraging for breakfast (which they were careful to pay for), Colonel Smith and his officers relaxed under a tree by the millpond. From time to time they sent across the road to Wright's Tavern for food and drink.

The liberty pole crashed down under the axes of the grenadiers. Soldiers took the fragments of the pole and some dismantled wooden gun carriages and made a bonfire near the Town Hall. A light breeze had sprung up, and the flames swung so close to the building that an old housekeeper ran up with a bucket of water. "Don't worry, mother," one of the officers told her, but another officer took pity on her puny effort and ordered the soldiers to douse the blaze. As they did so, black clouds of smoke began to billow up from the creosoted gun carriages.

During this time Captain Parsons had marched his light infantry over the North Bridge. The captain's orders were to secure the bridge and then to search the Barrett farm two miles away where, it was said, most of the Concord ammunition was stored. Parsons led four companies past the motionless minutemen and along the dirt track to the farm. He left the other three companies at the bridge in charge of Captain Walter Laurie.

Laurie stationed one company at the far end of the bridge and deployed the other two along a range of low hills a quarter of a mile away. The redcoats at the bridge—there were only thirty-five of them—and the Yankee militiamen on their hillock watched each other impassively, neither anxious to make the first hostile gesture.

So they might have stayed, prudently wary, if the smoke from the bonfire near the Town Hall had not begun to billow up over the treetops. "Will you let them burn the town down?" Joseph Hosmer called out hoarsely, pointing to the dark coils of smoke. The others shouted back that they would not. At the least they would march back across the bridge and put out the fire.

Two by two, filing down the slope in formation, the four hundred minutemen began to move slowly toward the bridgehead. To the isolated company of redcoats these determined farmers seemed overwhelming. Young Captain Laurie was uncertain just what to do, and in his uncertainty did nothing until the minutemen were almost on him. Colonel Barrett ordered his men to load their muskets but kept warning them not to fire unless the regulars fired first. With the advance of the militia files, the two nearby light infantry companies moved from their hill positions to reinforce the company at the bridge. Their arrival brought the number of British to one hundred.

Reeling under the heavy fire of minutemen across the North Bridge, Captain Laurie's light infantry (right) begins its undisciplined flight back to Concord. A Concord youth, who took no part in the skirmish, later used an axe to kill the wounded redcoat shown falling near the stone wall in Doolittle's engraving.

Belatedly Laurie led his men back across the narrow footbridge. Several of his soldiers began tearing up the planking. The rest, instead of taking up firing positions, remained bunched at the far end. Laurie sent a desperate message to Colonel Smith for reinforcements. The militia were now sixty yards from the bridge, headed by Major Buttrick and the eager young leader of the Acton company, Isaac Davis. Colonel Barrett, watching on horseback from the high ground in the rear, repeated his order not to fire.

Then some nervous finger pressed a trigger and the inevitable provoking shot rang out. As at Lexington, no one would ever be certain who fired, but it seems probable that it was one of the undisciplined light infantrymen. The shot was followed by the crash of a British volley. As the acrid powder smoke swirled across the bridge, the minutemen stopped short. Isaac Davis and another man of the Acton company lay dead on the ground. Major Buttrick, forgetting in the heat of the moment the precision of military command, called out desperately, "Fire, for God's sake, fire!"

The minutemen's return volley swept the bridge. Three redcoats were killed instantly and eight or ten others wounded. The rest bolted toward Concord, in spite of Captain Laurie's furious efforts to stop them. Halfway there the fear-struck redcoats met Colonel Smith on the road—late once more—with a reinforcing company of grenadiers, and he led them back to the village.

Smith seemed bewildered. For two hours after the bridge engagement he could not make up his mind what to do. The British wounded were casually forgotten, as was Captain Parsons and his four companies at the Barrett farm. Smith ordered his troops into line, then dismissed them, and a few minutes later reassembled them to march a few yards before dismissing them again. Nine hours before, he had sent a message to General Gage asking for reinforcements; while he delayed, he no doubt hoped they would arrive. But the minutemen were swarming on the outskirts of Concord like hornets from a kicked nest. The longer the English commander delayed, the more colonials he would have to face.

News of the bloodshed at Lexington Common had spread through the countryside. For thirty miles around men were leaving their ploughs and their axes and their workshops and heading for Concord. Colonel Barrett's militia had crossed the North Bridge after the British flight and now lay concealed behind stone walls on the next hill. From their cover, on all sides, the minutemen watched the indecisive regulars.

The battered British expedition was rescued at Lexington by Lord Percy, whose regiment was later cut to pieces during the battle at Breed's Hill. Thomas Gainsborough painted this portrait of the handsome Englishman.

The Yankee farmers were no longer the hesitant militia of the early morning. Anger possessed them now, as it possessed the Lexington minutemen under Captain Parker; they came marching up the Concord road with a fifer shrilling the old revolutionary tune, *The White Cockade.*

Meanwhile, Captain Parsons and his four companies of redcoats had made their way back to the common unmolested. At noon, Colonel Smith at last gave the belated order to return to Boston. Moving out over the road they had covered in such gay spirits a few hours earlier, the British columns now marched mutely, fifes and drums silenced.

The grenadiers kept to the road, surrounding the walking wounded; the more seriously wounded rode on horseback. The light infantry marched as flankers along the ridge to the left and the meadows to the right. Nothing happened until they reached Meriam's Corner, a mile down the Lexington road.

At the corner the road narrowed to a small bridge over a brook. Beyond that bridge—behind houses, barns, walls, any shelter they could find—the minutemen waited with loaded muskets. As the light infantry flankers closed in and the columns drew together, the concealed minutemen opened up a withering if irregular fire. The baffled redcoats could see no target to reply to. "They were waylaid and a grait Many killed," wrote Amos Barrett, the young minuteman who had so enjoyed the early morning fifing. "When I got there a grait many Lay dead and the Road was bloddy."

From behind a boulder a muzzle protruded briefly, a Yankee farmer took careful aim, and a redcoat dropped. The landscape seemed alive with such invisible riflemen. A young British officer thought there must have been about 5,000 of them. When one minuteman company had used up its ammunition, another company appeared just down the road. The way to Lexington was a six-mile gantlet, with a hail of bullets scoring the regulars on both sides.

Aimlessly the redcoats fired back, their spirits ebbing with each mile. Colonel Smith was shot in the leg, but he was so conspicuous a target on horseback that he preferred to dismount and limp along on foot. As his troops neared Lexington, discipline gave way to despair. The light infantrymen huddled in the road now, exhausted from their flanking efforts. Even the hardier grenadiers began to waver. Each wall and shrub and tree seemed to spit fire. Scarlet-coated bodies sprawled in the dust. Finally, as the white buildings of Lexington glimmered through the trees, the soldiers broke into a panic, no longer an army but a fleeing mob.

If Gage's relief expedition had not reached Lexington at this crucial moment, Smith's battered and broken force would have had to choose between surrender and annihilation. But the relief was there: the 1st brigade—

On the brink of destruction, Colonel Smith's exhausted troops (seen at right) march toward Lord Percy's relief column drawn up (left center) near Lexington. Doolittle shows the two officers conferring on horseback, while the ever-present minutemen keep up a continual fire from behind a wall in the foreground.

three regiments of infantry, a battalion of marines, and a detachment of royal artillery—under the command of an alert, highly-professional soldier, thirty-two-year-old Hugh, Earl Percy.

Percy, delayed by army red tape in setting out, first learned of Smith's predicament at Menotomy and at once speeded up his march to Lexington. At the edge of town, after taking in the situation in one quick, careful glance, he set up his advance line on high ground along the Boston road, half a mile from the village. On hills to the right and left he placed fieldpieces—cannon called six-pounders from the weight of their shot. One fieldpiece was in easy range of the common. Percy then deployed his soldiers to form a large square fronting on the road with the sides running up the hills that lay parallel to it. Within this well-chosen site, guarded by sharpshooters and by fieldpieces, Smith's soldiers could find safety.

The beaten redcoats fleeing up the road cried out in relief when they saw Percy's brigade, stumbled into the protection of the square, and collapsed in the meadow grass. Percy sent a few warning cannon shots against the eagerly pursuing minutemen. The colonials, although uninjured, were impressed, particularly when a cannon ball cut through one side of the meetinghouse and came out the other. With the artillerymen commanding the heights, the Yankees

Paul Revere was both courier and printer for the Massachusetts Committee of Safety. The thrifty colony paid his 1775 bill only after cutting Revere's courier fee by 20 per cent.

kept their distance and held little councils out of range. They were cheered by the appearance of Dr. Joseph Warren, who had heard the news in Boston and rode out just behind Percy's force. But they came no closer to the British square.

Percy was no dilatory Colonel Smith, and he knew that the four-hour march back would be full of hazard. Carefully he made his preparations, rightly convinced that he need fear no frontal attacks. He gave Smith's men a half hour's rest, then formed them up at the head of his column—the most protected place. At 3:45 P.M. he gave the signal to set out.

The long column of regulars wound along the dusty road and over the hills like a great scarlet snake. Percy was careful to put out extended flanking parties on either side. He issued his orders—snipers to be killed if caught; houses harboring snipers to be burned; the cannon to be unlimbered in case of heavy attack.

Following Percy's 1,800 men, fanning out through woods and fields, came an equal number of minutemen. British flankers moving behind the cover of stone walls occasionally ambushed some of them. The hidden musketry continued, but the shots, now coming from a greater distance, were less effective.

At Menotomy, where the land grew flatter, the regulars were able to fire back with some success. Minutemen kept flocking in from the towns near Boston; in all, perhaps 3,500 were involved that day. When they showed signs of pressing too close, Percy checked them with cannon fire. Houses in the line of march were sacked or destroyed. A number of minutemen and several bystanders were killed along the way. By the time the regulars reached Cambridge they were tiring, the flankers almost done in. Still the minutemen peppered them with shot.

It was eight by the time Lord Percy was able to lead his men to the safety of Charlestown Neck, where a protective line was at once set up. The minutemen had no intention of fighting face to face in battle order, and they decided to call it a day. Counting up all of their losses, the British listed 73 killed, 174 wounded, and 26 missing. The colonials had 49 killed, 39 wounded, and 5 missing. Lord Percy appraised his opponents with cool military respect. "Whoever looks upon them as an irregular mob," he wrote, "will find himself much mistaken."

While the shots echoed at Concord and Lexington, Benjamin Franklin—long-time agent in London for Pennsylvania, Georgia, New Jersey, and Massachusetts—was somewhere in the mid-Atlantic on his way back from England. Still in his mind and heart was the idea of a union of all the colonies, self-governing, self-regulating, yet united by ties of blood and friendship with the mother country. In Franklin's belief this commonwealth of nations would be the most impressive political combination in the world.

Until Lexington and Concord, Franklin's vision of empire was a real possibility. Even men like Dr. Warren would still consider it for some time to come. But on that day of bloodshed and death in two obscure Massachusetts villages, a page of history had been turned forever.

English settlers fighting for their rights as Englishmen—so the minutemen at the North Bridge had seen themselves. There were not many doctrinaire revolutionaries among them. Many had fought in the French and Indian Wars as Englishmen—under Wolfe at Quebec, under young Lord Howe at Ticonderoga, or before the sea-fringed walls of the Louisbourg

fortress. But in that one fatal moment when Major Buttrick—hesitating perhaps before its very enormity—gave the command to fire on the redcoats they had once marched with, those Yankee farmers and tradesmen were no longer discontented colonial subjects of King George III. They had become Americans.

Alonzo Chappel's romantic painting shows the full fury of the minutemen's attack on the fleeing redcoats. To protect themselves against snipers, the British set fire to several houses near the road, one of which burns at right. In his report Lord Percy wrote, "There was not a stone-wall or house . . . from whence the Rebels did not fire upon us."

A LIST of the Names of the PROVINCIALS who were Killed and Wounded in the late Engagement with His Majesty's Troops at *Concord*, &c.

KILLED.

Of *Lexington*.
*Mr. Robert Munroe,
*Mr. Jonas Parker,
*Mr. Samuel Hadley,
*Mr. Jonas Harrington,
*Mr. Caleb Harrington,
*Mr. Isaac Muzzy,
*Mr. John Brown,
Mr. John Raymond,
Mr. Nathaniel Wyman,
Mr. Jedediah Munroe.

Of *Menotomy*.
Mr. Jason Russel,
Mr. Jabez Wyman,
Mr. Jason Winship.

Of *Sudbury*.
Deacon Haynes,
Mr. —— Reed.

Of *Concord*.
Capt. James Miles.

Of *Bedford*.
Capt. Jonathan Willson.

Of *Acton*.
Capt. Davis,
Mr. —— Hosmer,
Mr. James Howard.

Of *Woburn*.
*Mr. Azael Porter,
Mr. Daniel Thompson.

Of *Charlestown*.
Mr. James Miller,
Capt. William Barber's Son.

Of *Brookline*.
Isaac Gardner, Esq;

Of *Cambridge*.
Mr. John Hicks,
Mr. Moses Richardson,
Mr. William Massey.

Of *Medford*.
Mr. Henry Putnam.

Of *Lynn*.
Mr. Abednego Ramsdell,
Mr. Daniel Townsend,
Mr. William Flint,
Mr. Thomas Hadley.

Of *Danvers*.
Mr. Henry Jacobs,
Mr. Samuel Cook,
Mr. Ebenezer Goldthwait,
Mr. George Southwick,
Mr. Benjamin Daland, jun.
Mr. Jotham Webb,
Mr. Perley Putnam.

Of *Salem*.
Mr. Benjamin Peirce.

WOUNDED.

Of *Lexington*.
Mr. John Robbins,
Mr. John Tidd,
Mr. Solomon Peirce,
Mr. Thomas Winship,
Mr. Nathaniel Farmer,
Mr. Joseph Comee,
Mr. Ebenezer Munroe,
Mr. Francis Brown,
Prince Easterbrooks,
(A Negro Man.

Of *Framingham*.
Mr. —— Hemenway.

Of *Bedford*.
Mr. John Lane.

Of *Woburn*.
Mr. George Reed,
Mr. Jacob Bacon.

Of *Medford*.
Mr. William Polly.

Of *Lynn*.
Mr. Joshua Felt,
Mr. Timothy Munroe.

Of *Danvers*.
Mr. Nathan Putnam,
Mr. Dennis Wallis.

Of *Beverly*.
Mr. Nathaniel Cleaves.

MISSING.

Of *Menotomy*.
Mr. Samuel Frost,
Mr. Seth Russell.

Those distinguished with this Mark [*] were killed by the first Fire of the Regulars.

Sold in Queen-Street.

From Concord to Lexington
Mr. Deacon Mr. Loeings Mr. Mulikens Mr. B——
Published according to Act June 19 1775

The bloody incidents at Lexington and Concord provided excellent ammunition for American propagandists. The broadside at left, listing the names of those provincials killed and wounded during the engagements, was obviously designed to attract the sympathies of colonists whose loyalty to the mother country was wavering. In the cartoon above, a satirist has portrayed British troops as cowards with donkey heads retreating through Lexington, some of them looting the buildings they have set afire. They are being chased by minutemen whose officer says, "Come on my Brave Boys, let us Die or be free."

The coat of arms of George III

2

Rising of the Wind

When, on September 8, 1760, the Marquis de Vaudreuil surrendered Montreal to the armies of Major General Jeffery Amherst and ceded Canada to the British crown, it marked the end of seventy years of intermittent war. New England farmers could now sleep untroubled by thoughts of war whoops and midnight murder. Settlers in upper New York and Pennsylvania needed worry no longer about the fierce and bloody Indian raids from the north. At last the French-Indian challenge had been met.

The first reaction among the colonists was a surge of good will and affection for the mother country. Amherst seemed as much a hero in America as he did in England. In Boston his victory was celebrated with a parade of militiamen, a dinner at Faneuil Hall, thundering cannon salutes, and long sermons from every pulpit in the province. His withdrawal from Canada to winter quarters in New York was one long triumphant parade. On the evening of the general's arrival the entire city was brilliantly illuminated in his honor. He was met by the mayor and the aldermen and a committee of citizens who presented him with a gold snuffbox on which was engraved in Latin, "Conqueror of the Canadian Gauls."

That October George II died, and the dull, well-intentioned, authoritarian George III came to the throne. At first he was popular. Bonfires blazed across America and on the hills of England in honor of his accession, and the young king's health was drunk in every tavern.

This attachment of Americans to the king survived their many differences of opinion with the English government and lasted among many right up to the Revolution. It was the king's ministers who were at fault, they said, not the king himself. New Englanders still felt that way when they referred to the redcoats at Lexington and Concord as the "ministerial" rather than the "royal" troops. As late as 1770 the Sons of Liberty could announce in Boston, "We are rebels against Parliament—we adore the king."

By the end of the French and Indian Wars many of the colonists were of the third or fourth American generation. To them the memory of the mother country had become remote, blurred. London and its court could scarcely be imagined by New England farmers or Pennsylvania frontiersmen going about their long day's tasks. A new land with its new climate and new ways of life was creating a new type of person. Just as the design of a brick or stone English cottage became in America a cottage of wood, so the transplanted Englishman became something else without being wholly aware of it himself.

What was good for England was not necessarily good for America. That was the lesson to be learned after the last French war. America and England then were like two friends walking together, yet on opposite sides of a small brook. At first, it was still possible for each of them to jump to the other bank. But as they walked farther, the brook widened into a stream that could be waded only with some difficulty. Then the stream turned into a river. The figures on the opposite banks grew smaller, and when the river finally became a tidal inlet, they were lost to each other, divided for good.

For all the heroes and villains, wise men and fools, who helped make the history of that era, the chief cause of the American Revolution was that the interests of the colonists and the interests of the mother country grew too far apart. And when it became apparent that these differences could not or would not be bridged, the Revolution was unavoidable.

By the time that the peace treaty between France and England was finally signed in 1763, the glitter of Amherst's victory was tarnished by thoughts of the war debt. It was the costliest war that England had ever fought, and to Englishmen it seemed only just that the colonists should contribute their share of the expense.

METROPOLITAN MUSEUM OF ART

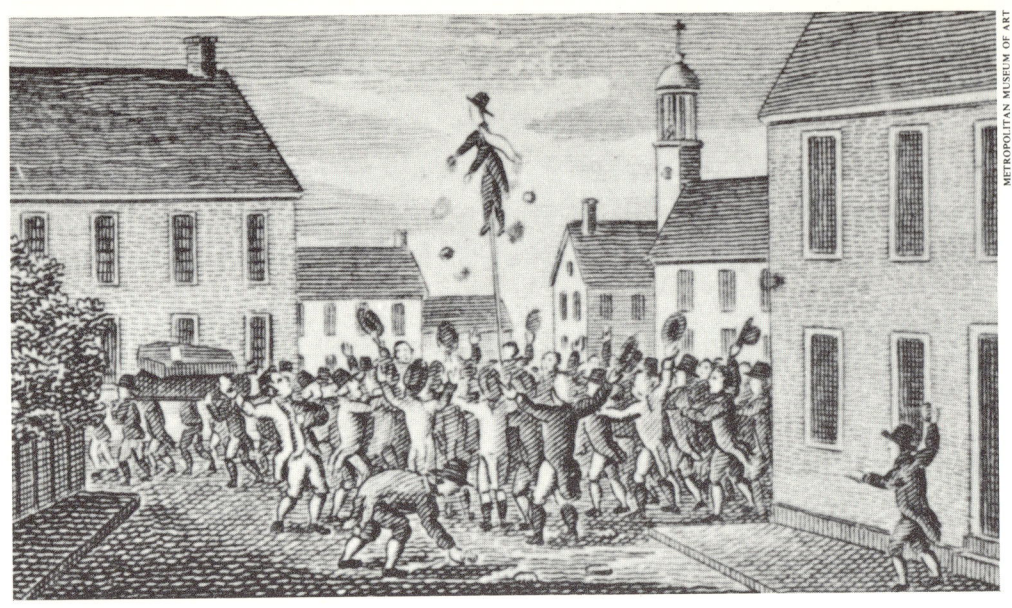

Chancellor of the Exchequer George Grenville's persistence in levying the stamp tax aroused bitterness throughout the colonies. In the old woodcut above, New Hampshire townspeople hang a tax collector in effigy.

At first colonists blamed the British Parliament, not the king, for the restrictions on their liberties. Actually, the House of Commons, shown below during a debate, was controlled by George III and his ministers.

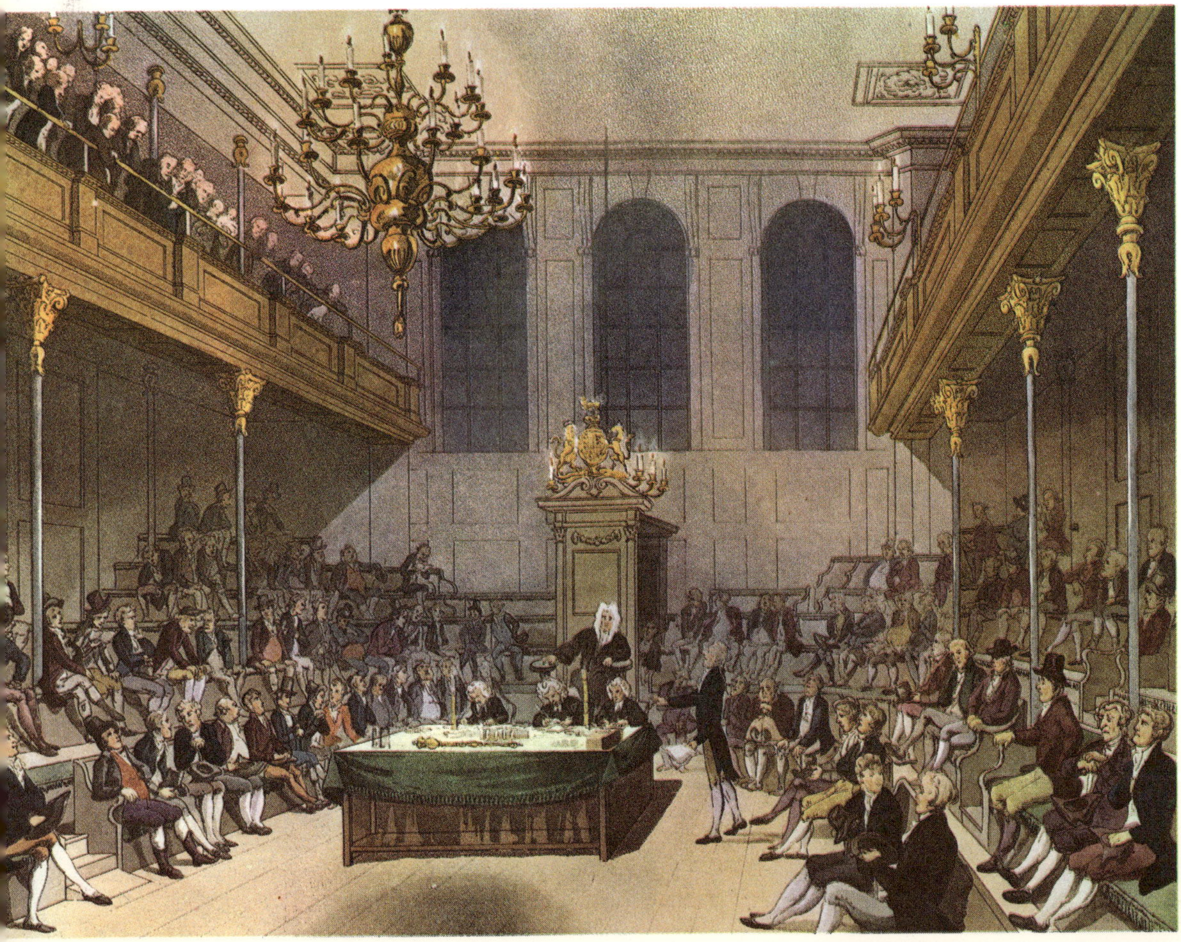

The Microcosm of London: CULVER PICTURES

By British standards the colonies seemed lightly taxed. In England, as just one example, there was a tax on windows that in 1761 was expanded to include even the humblest cottage. Even today one can see occasional eighteenth-century English houses with the outlines of windows that had been bricked up to avoid the tax.

For over one hundred years the American colonists had never paid direct taxes except by vote of their own assemblies, and they had come to feel that only their own assemblies had the right to levy such taxes. Englishmen, however, felt that Parliament, as the central governing body of the empire, had the right to control and tax any part of that empire.

In 1764 Parliament passed a series of resolutions to raise money in North America to help meet the expense of defending the region. The fifteenth of these resolutions—to be known as the Stamp Act—called for the levying of stamp duties. This meant that all newspapers, legal documents, wills, mortgages, business papers—even boxes of playing cards and dice—had to have duty stamps pasted on them.

Such stamps had been in general use in England since the previous century. George Grenville, the British Chancellor of the Exchequer, honestly thought that such stamps would be the easiest and most painless way of collecting taxes in the colonies—especially since all the money collected would be spent in North America.

The colonists thought otherwise, and they thought so violently, particularly because of the business depression that had followed the wartime boom. "Taxation without representation is tyranny!" became their shouted slogan. But their deepest objection was to the novelty of the tax. They had always been indirectly taxed by the mother country through duties and excises, but this was the first time they had ever been required to pay direct taxes to the British government.

Such a state of affairs was unheard of, and—as Grenville might have realized had he been more astute—they were outraged. Effigies of the chancellor were soon being burned from Quebec to Georgia, and it was emphatically hinted that if he cared to cross the ocean he would find a gallows ready for him. Before long the colonies were seething with secret societies calling themselves the Sons of Liberty, whose purpose was to nullify the Stamp Act. One of the most unexpected results of this act was that it brought the disunited colonies together for the first time. In October, 1765, delegates from nine colonies met in New York to organize a single protest by forming the Stamp Act Congress.

Grenville still persisted, determined to show those malcontents across the Atlantic that Parliament had the *right* to lay a direct, internal tax on the colonies. With the shortsighted disregard of colonial opinion that was to become increasingly characteristic of the British government in its relations with North America, the Grenville ministry persuaded itself that once the Stamp Act was firmly applied, the colonists would have to accept it. Bales of duty stamps were prepared for shipment overseas, and a stamp director was appointed in each colony to take charge of the stamps and see that they were distributed.

As soon as the fateful news crossed the Atlantic the colonies were in an uproar. Although the stamp directors were respectable and prominent colonists, neither their respectability nor their prominence helped them against the mob opposition directed by the Sons of Liberty.

In Massachusetts the rumor flashed about that the new official would be Andrew Oliver, secretary of the colony and brother-in-law of Lieutenant Governor Thomas Hutchinson. The next morning effigies of Oliver and the devil were found hanging on a great elm on the corner of the present Washington and Essex streets in Boston. From then on, the elm was known as the Liberty Tree, forerunner of liberty trees and liberty poles in towns and villages throughout the colonies. That evening a surly, hooting mob took down Oliver's effigy, paraded it in front of his town house, and beheaded it. Then, with rising excitement, the mob began to stone the windows and finally broke down the door and stormed inside to look for the luckily absent secretary.

There were similar wild scenes in the other colonies and even as far away as the placid Bahama Islands. In Newport, the Rhode Island stamp director, after he was hanged in effigy and forced to take shelter on a British warship in the harbor, announced that he was quite willing to resign. New York mobs broke into their stamp director's house, smashed his furniture, stole his silver, and drank his wine. Then they marched through the streets with effigies of Governor Cadwallader Colden and the devil. These they finally placed in the governor's coach, which they hauled away to make a bonfire.

In Pennsylvania and Virginia, the stamp directors resigned with equal promptness when faced by mobs. In Nassau, the capital of the Bahamas, a crowd seized the local director and dragged him to a graveyard where they put him in a coffin, nailed down the lid, and lowered him into a shallow grave. When someone threw a handful of earth on the coffin, the distributor (whose name is lost to history) resigned.

Disregarding the overseas turmoil, Grenville was stubbornly resolved to enforce his Stamp Act. It is possible that the American Revolution might have broken out ten years earlier if he had not been forced from office by one of those quick changes in British politics. He was replaced by a new ministry under Lord Rockingham, who decided to yield and repeal the act. The colonies had indeed won their point, but it had taken mob action to do it.

Today it is difficult for us to under-

Furious criticism of the Stamp Act on both sides of the Atlantic forced its repeal in early 1766. This English satire appeared shortly afterward, depicting Grenville (left center) carrying the coffin of his defeated policy, while in the background a sign proclaims "Goods NOW Ship'd for America."

stand the power of the streets two hundred years ago, when mobs were able to take virtual control of a city and to defy and in some cases almost break a government. We are used to uniformed policemen or soldiers trained and ready to break up threatening demonstrations.

In the eighteenth century it was very different. Sometimes the mob actually ruled, as during the French Revolution. In London in 1780 a mob stormed out of the slums to burn and loot whole sections of the city in protest against the Catholic Relief Bill.

This 1769 woodcut shows the kind of carriage used in the Boston Pope's Day celebrations. A resident noted that in one long series of riots "the North End Pope was never taken but once, and then the Captain had been early wounded...."

During those so-called Gordon Riots it took General Amherst and the regular army almost a week to restore order, and over 450 Londoners died in the streets.

A chief reason for such mobs was that the cities lacked any police force. Beyond a few ineffectual constables, there was no organized protection, nor would there be until the next century. For a long time most citizens felt that a uniformed police force patrolling the streets would be an outrage against individual freedom. Consequently, whenever a mob decided to storm the king's palace in France, or in London to force members of Parliament to kneel in the mud, or across the Atlantic to pillage a stamp distributor's town house or burn a royal governor's coach, there was no one to interfere. Unless there were soldiers nearby, and a commander willing to take the responsibility for calling them out to clear the streets, there was no way of controlling an eighteenth-century mob.

The most savage mobs were found in the seaports, swarming in the network of mean streets near the harbor. Here were sailors, deserters, roisterers, toughs, and a dozen varieties of troublemakers, itching for any kind of a fight and waiting only for a leader to give them a reason and show them the way.

On November 4, 1605, in London, thirty-six barrels of powder were discovered hidden in the vaults of one of the houses of Parliament. A group of conspirators had plotted to blow up the king and Parliament the following day in revenge for the strict penal laws against Catholics. Guy Fawkes, the man chosen to light the powder fuse, was arrested near the vaults. Ever since, and down to the present, November 5 has been celebrated in England as Guy Fawkes Day, with festivities and fireworks.

The celebration soon crossed the Atlantic to New England, where it became known as Pope's Day. In many ways it resembled the later Halloween. Each town built a large float called a pope's carriage on which were comic figures of a pope, a devil, and any currently unpopular political figures. In the evening the float, illuminated by paper lanterns and with dancers and fiddlers on its platform, was dragged through the streets under the command of a captain. It was followed by a procession of boys and young men beating drums, ringing bells, and blowing whistles, and as it came to the wealthier houses it stopped for an early version of trick-or-treat. The increasingly rowdy celebration ended with a bonfire in which the various figures were burned along with fences and washtubs stolen on the way.

In Boston, Pope's Day became less a carnival than a vicious outlet for mob spirits. There were two pope's carriages in the town, one belonging to a North End gang, the other to one in the South End. When these gangs met on the evening of Pope's Day and the rival carriages faced each other, each gang set out to capture the other's pope. The result was a savage street battle in which many were injured and some were even killed. For twenty-four hours, to the dismay of respectable citizens and contrary to all law, Boston was in the hands of the mob.

It was Samuel Adams who first conceived of reconciling the two gangs and directing their mob impulses to political ends. Adams, born in 1722, was by this time a middle-aged man who looked far older than his years. His hair was sparse and gray, and his hands—even at times his voice—trembled. His clothes were seedy, and he looked the failure that in most respects he was; he had failed working for his father and failed working for himself, failed even in supporting his family. When he somehow managed to get himself elected tax collector, Adams nearly went to jail for his carelessness in the handling of public funds.

His life, and the only thing he really cared about, was politics, and for politics he showed a superb, relentless talent. Long before most of the colonists had given the idea a thought, Sam Adams was considering methods of bringing about a complete separation of the new America and the old mother country. Adams was not just

Some of his fellow politicians considered John Hancock (above) vain and arrogant, but the rich Boston merchant's support lent great prestige to the Whig cause. Hancock's portrait and the one opposite were painted by John Singleton Copley.

Sam Adams, pointing to the Massachusetts charter (left), sought to push the colonies into open conflict with England. He was supremely talented as an agitator, but his power declined during the Revolution when such qualities were no longer needed.

against King George III; he opposed all kings everywhere. He disliked an aristocracy, a government of betters, whether royal or republican. His ideal was a frugal republic of few luxuries in which all men were roughly equal—a republic resembling the ancient Sparta he had read about in Plutarch's *Lives*. With this idea firmly fixed in his head and working with a group of the Sons of Liberty known as the "Loyall Nine," he came to dominate and control the mob that terrorized Boston during the Revolutionary period. Sam Adams was the "mob master."

Even when the gangs were still acting on their own, as in the sack of the Oliver house, Adams had established close and friendly relations with the leaders. And he must have been more than aware of what was brewing when the mob broke loose two weeks later and gutted Lieutenant Governor Hutchinson's mansion.

Thomas Hutchinson was one of the wealthiest men forming the group around the royal governor. A holder of many offices, he was a member of the Governor's Council and chief justice of the province as well as lieutenant governor. His mansion was the handsomest in the town, and to demonstrate the Hutchinson loyalty the crown of England was carved in the stone lintel over each window.

Hutchinson—no friend of the Stamp Act—was a scholar as well as a statesman, and his *History of the Colony of Massachusetts Bay* endures as one of the most important documents in the early history of New England. But for all his abilities he lacked the common touch, and as the crisis grew so did the feeling against him.

It was on August 26, 1765—the hot-

MAP DIVISION, N.Y. PUBLIC LIBRARY

When Boston (right) fell under the control of the mob, Governor Bernard fled to Castle William (center). The fort was later destroyed during the British evacuation.

test day in the year—that the mob finally went for him. Early in the evening a group had lighted a bonfire in King Street near the Old State House. A restless crowd soon gathered, and in a short time whistles and horns began to sound the mob call that sent the strong-arm squads swarming out of their taverns and garrets. Liquor, always plentiful in such circumstances, became even more plentiful as the mob broke into the houses and cellars of several customs officials. Then the name Hutchinson began to be passed about in the hot darkness, and with joyful rage the cry went up: "Pull down the chief justice's house!"

Hutchinson was warned that the mob was after him. He escaped just as the axes began to swing against his front door. "The hellish crew fell upon my house with the rage of devils," he wrote afterward. Through the formal, ornamented rooms the looters and the wreckers stormed their way.

Everything that could not be carried off was destroyed—family portraits, busts of the king and queen, rugs, clocks, china, books, even the wall paneling. The wine cellar was the first to go. In the garden the flower beds were trampled and the fruit trees leveled. The manuscript of the second volume of Hutchinson's *History*—the first had just been published a few months earlier—was hurled into the gutter and trampled in the mud along with all the early records of the colony that he had collected. Fortunately, the manuscript and many of the records were later gathered up and returned to the lieutenant governor, but of his house nothing remained except "bare walls and floors."

The first reaction of Sam Adams and his Loyall Nine to the night of destruction was sudden uneasiness about what steps the English government might take against this reckless challenge of authority. Adams now called the gutting of the Hutchinson mansion a "high-handed Enormity" and maintained that it had been committed by "vagabound Strangers." It was at this point that Adams set out to bring the mobsters under firm and more disciplined control by sending in among them artisans of a "superior set" to act as controlling noncommissioned officers. They came to be called Adams' Mohawks.

The Sons of Liberty and their mob adherents became the unofficial rulers of Boston. Governor Francis Bernard and many of his officials thought it wiser to retire to the safety of Castle William in Boston harbor, under the protection of the cannon of British men-of-war. Customs officials who made any effort to enforce the laws had a rough time.

Finally, even the English politicians had to realize that the Stamp Act was unenforceable. It was repealed by Rockingham's ministry in the spring of 1766. The colonies celebrated the repeal as a public holiday. In Boston an enormous framed obelisk, large enough to hold three hundred lighted lamps and covered with oiled paper,

was set up on the common. The four sides of the obelisk were covered with symbolic pictures and verses, and after it had blazed all night it was carted off to the Liberty Tree.

Whatever the fate of the Stamp Act, Parliament and most Englishmen still felt that the colonies were not paying their way. The spring of 1767 brought Charles Townshend in as Chancellor of the Exchequer. He was a reckless if brilliant politician who was said to have every talent but common sense. In the Townshend Acts he gave his name to a new and more indirect way of taxing the colonies. His acts proposed to place a duty on all imports to America of glass, paper, paint, and tea.

Since the colonists had long paid other duties with no undue protest, Parliament seemed to feel that there would be no objection to the modest duties of the Townshend Acts. Parliament could not have been more wrong. Coming so soon after the Stamp Act, the new acts caused widespread resentment across the Atlantic. Colonies got

In 1768 a powerful squadron of Royal Navy ships, "their cannon loaded . . . as for a regular siege," sailed into Boston harbor carrying troops to garrison the strife-torn city. This painting, by an American sailor named Christian Remick, shows part of the large force landing at Long Wharf (foreground).

together among themselves and agreed not to buy and not to import British goods. Bringing in only negligible revenues, the acts soon began to cost London merchants and exporters vast sums of money.

In Boston a town meeting was called to urge the inhabitants to boycott all taxed items. Smuggling at once increased, as did the violence against customs officers. In the summer of 1768 John Hancock's sleek sloop *Liberty* was caught in Boston harbor with her hold full of contra-

British cartoonists often sympathized with the underpaid British soldiers serving in America. The 1775 engraving above shows a redcoat unable to support his family while plump Englishmen enjoy life at home.

Some of General Gage's troops had to be quartered in tents on Boston Common. In the engraving at right, made from Christian Remick's 1768 painting, the 29th regiment drills before the Hancock mansion.

band wine by the British frigate *Romney*. At once the Sons of Liberty staged a "liberty riot" in protest. Governor Bernard, still ensconced in Castle William, wrote pleadingly to England that only the sending of soldiers could "rescue the Government from the hands of a trained mob and restore the activity of the Civil power."

In reply the home government dispatched seven transports and ships-of-war from Halifax. Although Sam Adams made great threats about what would happen to any arriving troops, on October 1, 1768, two regiments of infantry and an artillery company disembarked uneventfully at Boston's Long Wharf. They marched up King Street with drums beating and flags flying. The Sons of Liberty opposition collapsed like a pricked balloon.

Yet formidable as the redcoats appeared marching in precise lines, they seemed less than formidable as indi-

52

viduals. For a man of the eighteenth century, soldiering was often the last resort. Army ranks were made up in great part of derelicts, jailbirds, vagabonds, and green country boys—the unwanted of the world. Drilled to an iron discipline, they were fierce fighters in a formal battle. Singly they were often rather puny men. So wretchedly were they paid that it was not long before they took to wandering the streets of Boston, begging for odd jobs. Sons of Liberty, reviving in spirits, took to jeering at them. The more daring small boys would let fly stones or snowballs at passing red backs. A number of the soldiers deserted and melted away into the New England landscape. Those who were caught were hanged on Boston Common.

With British squads patrolling the streets of the occupied town, with sentries pacing back and forth in front of the Old State House, some sort of bloody clash between the redcoats and the citizens was—as Sam Adams well realized—inevitable. Early in 1770 the clash occurred. It was to become known as the Boston Massacre.

No one enjoys a military occupation, and Sam Adams made it his full-time job to stir up feeling against the redcoats and to make life as painful as possible for them. He published and circulated throughout the colonies a *Journal of Events* which gave lurid and, for the most part, imaginary accounts of British "atrocities" against the gentle and harmless inhabitants of Boston. No man or woman was safe, Adams wrote, from the "bloody-backed rascals."

His Mohawks made a habit of brawling with the redcoats in taverns and alleys, particularly with the soldiers of the 29th regiment, who were noted for their short tempers and quick fists. Often the soldiers clashed with the ropemakers, Boston's toughest citizens. Both sides seemed to relish a good street fight.

By March, Boston still lay under a foot of snow. At the beginning of the month Adams and the Loyall Nine plastered the town with forged notices, supposedly put out by the British, that the troops were intending to attack the townspeople. As crude as this propaganda was, it was widely believed. The atmosphere in Boston grew tense; on the evening of March 5, it finally exploded.

It was a cold moonlit night. A single British soldier stood in his sentry box at the upper end of King Street near the Old State House. Soon a group of boys gathered across the street and, as they often did, began to jeer at the "lobster back" and pelt him with snowballs and chunks of ice. Then a crowd of adults formed and a ring began to close in on the sentry box.

The sentry stepped out and, amidst jeers, threatened to run through anyone who came near enough to his bayonet. A small boy darted toward him and received a glancing blow from the redcoat's musket butt, not enough to harm him or even to knock him down, but enough to set the crowd off. There were shouts that the sentry was murdering a child, then cries of "Kill him! Kill him!" The bell of the Old South Meeting House rang out like a fire alarm, and the fringes of the crowd were suddenly bolstered by several hundred hard-faced sailors, porters, and ropemakers, urged on by a mysterious stranger in a red cape and wig who may have been Sam Adams himself.

John Adams—Sam's more refined cousin from Braintree—later described the mob as "a motley rabble." Among the ringleaders were Crispus Attucks, James Caldwell, Samuel Gray, and Patrick Carr—four bully-

In Paul Revere's engraving of the Boston Massacre, the redcoats were hardly the "fierce Barbarians" he has labeled them; also, five men died, not seven as he states. In the background is the Old State House.

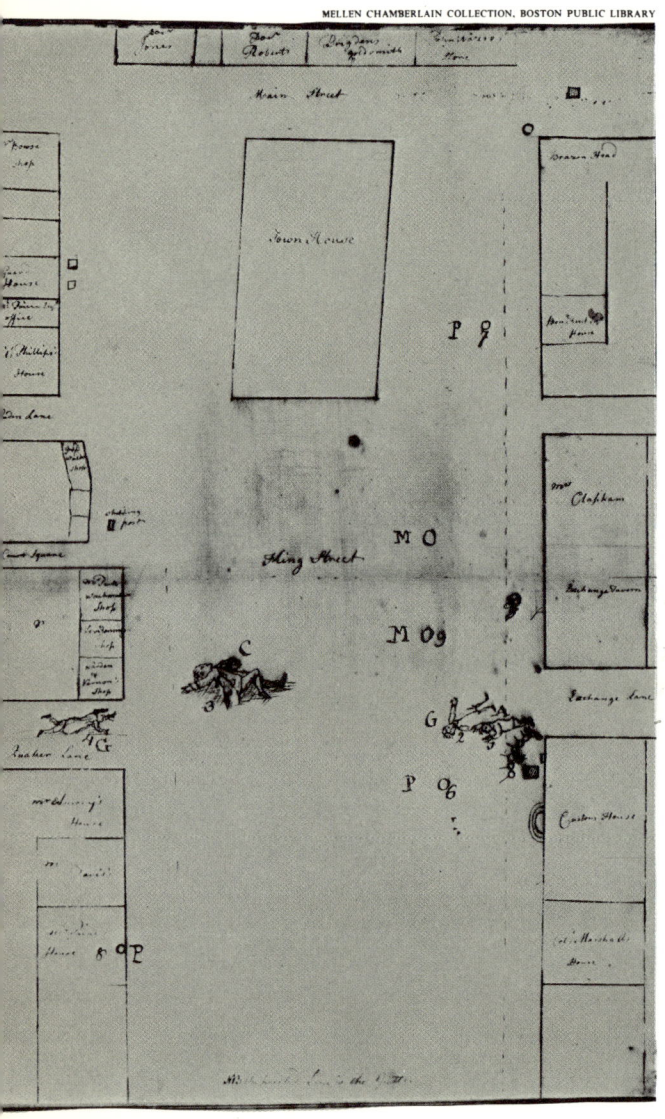

MELLEN CHAMBERLAIN COLLECTION, BOSTON PUBLIC LIBRARY

In contrast with his lurid engraving, Revere drew this accurate diagram of the Massacre for use at the soldiers' trial. The clash took place before the Custom House (right). The figure at far left is that of young Sam Maverick, an innocent bystander mortally wounded by a stray bullet.

boys who made a habit of drifting about town and attacking stray redcoats. Crispus Attucks was a dark giant of a man, part Negro, part Indian, part white; Gray was a ropemaker; Caldwell a ship's mate; and the Irish-born Carr an old hand at rioting.

As the din increased and the mob swarmed closer, Attucks thrust his club at the "lobster back" and said he would "have off one of his claws." Just before threatening hands reached him, the sentry called loudly, "Turn out the main guard!"

At once the duty officer, Captain John Preston, stepped out of the guardhouse across the street, followed by a guard of seven redcoats with fixed bayonets. They forced their way through the crowd and formed a semicircle around the sentry. As the threats increased, Preston ordered his men to prime and load. There was a hush while the iron ramrods rattled ominously in the musket barrels. The captain placed himself between the muskets and the crowd to keep his men from firing.

Some of the more sensible townspeople tried to urge the others to break up and go home. Instead, the surlier members of the mob pressed forward in a blind rush at the soldiers. Attucks struck Preston a blow with his club which nearly broke the officer's arm, then knocked down the sentry and tried to grab his musket. The rioters and soldiers struggled against each other. Then the fatal command rang out: "Fire!" As later at Lexington and Concord, no one knows who gave it. Preston did not. Possibly it was a mobster shouting in derision.

The shots echoed up and down the narrow street, and the panicking crowd tripped and fought its way back over the caked snow. The ground was littered with coats and hats and clubs—and here and there bodies. Captain Preston struggled to push the musket barrels up as he shouted to his men to hold their fire.

Attucks, Gray, and Caldwell lay dead in the snow. Patrick Carr and a young apprentice named Sam Maverick were mortally wounded; Carr lived long enough to confess remorsefully that he and his friends were to blame and that the redcoats had fired in self-defense.

The town and the surrounding countryside fumed with indignation. Most people at first were led to believe that the soldiers had fired without cause on harmless civilians. Overwhelmed by the protests, Lieutenant Governor Hutchinson had Preston and his men arrested and charged with murder. The British authorities even allowed the accused to be tried by a civilian court and a local jury.

It seemed that only a royal pardon could save the nine men from being hanged on Boston Common. So great was the feeling against the redcoats, and so great was the fear that the provincial militia would start pouring into the town, that Hutchinson reluctantly ordered the troops to Castle William. Once more the Sons of Liberty ruled the streets.

For Sam Adams the Massacre was a gift from heaven. At once his propaganda machine set to work extolling the King Street dead and calling for vengeance on the "redcoat butchers." His hot words resounded through the colonies. The dead bully-boys became martyrs to freedom, saints of liberty, the first blood shed against brute tyranny. Conspicuously absent from the list of martyrs was the name of Patrick Carr; his deathbed confession Adams explained away as that of an "Irish papist."

Adams' guiding hand can be seen in Paul Revere's famous engraving of the Massacre, where for all the crudeness of the drawing a myth is being created. Captain Preston grins evilly as he raises his sword in the command to fire. The soldiers aim point-blank at a group of citizens as mild-seeming and innocent as children.

There were other men in Boston, Whigs like the young lawyer Josiah Quincy and his colleague John Adams, who—though equally opposed to the English government—thought more of principle than they did of propaganda. Despite adverse public opinion, they agreed to defend Captain Preston and his men.

Quincy was twenty-six years old, hollow-faced, and failing in health if not in spirit. The roly-poly Adams was nine years older, a successful lawyer with a large practice. He was

The colonies moved a step closer to war in June, 1772, when a group of Rhode Island merchants seized and burned the British revenue cutter Gaspee, *which had grounded near Providence while chasing a smuggler. England was outraged by the incident; in America it was considered a protest against the king's tax policy.*

noted for his prudence and caution; yet when it came to the principle that every accused man has a right to be defended, no matter how unpopular his cause might be, John Adams threw caution to the wind.

Over Sam Adams' objections, Quincy and John Adams managed to get the trials delayed seven months. During that time the real story of what happened on the night of March 5 began to threaten the propaganda legend manufactured by Sam Adams —particularly after Carr's confession became known. Quincy and his partner took no chances. They saw to it that all the jurors were picked from outside Boston.

The trials were brief, the evidence extremely damaging to the Mohawks. In spite of the fact that the jury foreman was a Son of Liberty, Preston and six of his men were acquitted almost at once. The remaining two were found guilty of manslaughter and received the mild punishment—for that often-brutal era—of being branded on the hand.

Ironically, on the very day of the Boston Massacre, the English Cabinet in London agreed to drop all Townshend duties except the token tax on tea—and even the tea tax was retained by only one vote. After some initial protests the colonists came grudgingly to accept the tax. After all, tea was still cheaper than in England. Business was improving and many people had grown tired of Sam Adams and his disturbances.

Then in May, 1773, Parliament passed the Tea Act. This act gave the great East India Company a monopoly of sending and distributing tea to North America. The act allowed the company to set up warehouses in Boston, New York, Charleston, and Philadelphia for the sale of the tea.

American merchants and importers were dismayed and furious. Not only were they being cut out of their old profitable tea market, but they felt this might be just the beginning, with items other than tea to follow. Also, the company's high-grade tea was to sell for so little that those merchants who had been selling vast quantities of cheap smuggled bohea tea would soon be driven out of business. The Tea Act revived the drooping Sons of Liberty; more than that, it brought them into an alliance of anger with highly respected colonial merchants and importers.

Under Sam Adams' guidance the Massachusetts Bay Committee of Correspondence, which he had founded, called on all the colonies to prevent the East India tea from being landed in America. Mass meetings were held in the seaports. Again the Boston Sons of Liberty gathered under the Liberty Tree. New York

OVERLEAF: *The heart of Boston, shown here after the Revolution, had hardly changed since the 1770's. The Old State House (center) was the seat of Massachusetts government until nearly 1800. The Massacre took place at the red-brick Custom House (right).*
MASSACHUSETTS HISTORICAL SOCIETY

As the breach widened between England and America, colonial town meetings often turned into bitter disputes among loyal supporters of the king and patriots who demanded rebellion.

ship captains in London refused the tea as cargo.

Nevertheless, shipments were soon on their way to New York, Philadelphia, and Charleston. Three ships, loaded with 342 chests of tea valued at what would now be at least a half a million dollars, were sent to Boston where Governor Hutchinson's two sons had been appointed distributors. The Sons of Liberty swore that none of the tea would ever be unloaded.

At the end of November, 1773, the first of the tea ships, the *Dartmouth*, arrived in Boston harbor and tied up at Griffin's Wharf. She was followed shortly afterward by the *Beaver* and the *Eleanor*.

By Massachusetts law a cargo had to be unloaded within twenty days or sent back. The Sons of Liberty now threatened to tar and feather any captain who allowed his tea to be landed. So the chests remained in the holds.

Governor Hutchinson—once again driven to the safety of Castle William in the harbor—felt that the British government made a mistake in not repealing the original tea tax; he also felt that the Tea Act that followed was badly timed and probably futile. But he was determined to enforce the law against the mob.

Meanwhile, Sam Adams was leading turbulent protest meetings at Faneuil Hall, attended not only by Bostonians but by increasing numbers of Massachusetts farmers. Hutchinson lacked the power to disperse such rowdy meetings. Adams, with his

To the PUBLIC.

THE Senſe of the City relative to the Landing the India Company's Tea, being ſignified to Captain Lockyer, by the Committee, neverthelefs, it is the Defire of a Number of the Citizens, that at his Departure from hence, he ſhould ſee, with his own Eyes, their Deteſtation of the Meaſures purſued by the Miniſtry and the India Company, to enſlave this Country. This will be declared by the Convention of the People at his Departure from this City; which will be on next Saturday Morning, about nine o'Clock, when no Doubt, every Friend to this Country will attend. The Bells will give the Notice about an Hour before he embarks from Murray's Wharf.

By Order of the COMMITTEE.

NEW YORK, APRIL 21ſt, 1774.

A spirit of violent protest swept quickly through the colonies after the Tea Act was passed. Variations of the Boston Tea Party occurred in several coastal cities, whose merchants were greatly affected by the new bill. The 1774 broadside above, calling for a demonstration against the act, appeared in New York, where one tea ship was turned back and the cargo of another thrown unceremoniously into the harbor. The 1773 handbill below announces the arrival of a tea ship in Philadelphia.

Monday Morning, December 27, 1773.

THE Tea-Ship being arrived, every Inhabitant who wiſhes to preſerve the Liberty of America, is defired to meet at the STATE-HOUSE, This Morning, preciſely at TEN o'Clock, to adviſe what is beſt to be done on this alarming Criſis.

The Boston Tea Party was performed with incredible ease and simplicity. "We were surrounded by British armed ships," a participant recalled years later, "but no attempt was made to resist us." England's angry reply, the Boston Port Act, served only to unite the thirteen colonies against the mother country.

Committee of Correspondence and reinforced by his Mohawks, seemed to be running the town.

December 17, 1773, was the final day for the tea to be unloaded. On the afternoon of the sixteenth, several thousand excited Bostonians crowded into the Old South Meeting House to listen to firebrand speeches by Josiah Quincy, Sam Adams, and John Hancock; an even greater crowd milled about in a drizzling rain outside. While the vehement oratory rocked the rafters, a last message was sent to Governor Hutchinson, asking him to reconsider and let the tea ships sail away.

It was growing dark, and the Old South candles were being lit when the messenger returned with Hutchinson's refusal. Sam Adams, a mocking note of triumph in his voice, announced the refusal and added, "This meeting can do nothing more to save the country."

The announcement was a signal that set off a succession of war whoops outside. At once a band of 150 men disguised as Indians dashed out of Edes & Gill's print shop close by. Yelling wildly and brandishing hatchets, their faces smeared with paint and lampblack, they headed for the waterfront. The mob followed.

At Griffin's Wharf they swarmed over the tea ships, demanded the keys from the unresisting watch, and proceeded to haul tea chest after tea chest onto the decks and dump them into the harbor. One of the "Indians" remarked later that he had never worked harder in his life than he did that night. When the last of the tea was in the water, they formed ranks, shouldered their "tommyhawks," and marched behind a fifer to the Old State House. No one dared stand in their way.

The Boston Tea Party was, as Hutchinson himself admitted, "the boldest stroke which had yet been struck in America." This spectacular act of defiance electrified the colonies. Boston assumed the lead in resistance, becoming an example for the rest of North America. Sam Adams' tea party may well be considered the first act of the American Revolution. But if the colonies hailed it, in England it was considered an outrageous insult. Lord North, the new prime minister, felt that he could do no less than accept the challenge of Adams and his Mohawks.

With the usual bumbling disregard for American feelings—and indeed for American consequences—Lord North decided to close the port of Boston. He ignored the fact that this would surely unite the other colonies in sympathetic opposition. By the Boston Port Act, Parliament locked the town and emptied the harbor. Not even the ferry ran across the bay to Charlestown. On June 1, 1774, the day the bill went into effect, all the bells of Boston tolled in mourning.

Governor Hutchinson had by this time been recalled to England and replaced by General Gage, a man of unmilitary mildness who had long lived in America, and whose great concern in Boston was to keep his troops under control and avoid any incidents. Gage controlled the town, but the Sons of Liberty ran the countryside. The wealthier Tories—colonists loyal to the crown—began to hurry into Boston as the more prominent Whigs hurried out. Boston Common resounded to the commands of British drill sergeants.

Sympathy for the stagnating port was expressed in practical ways by other towns. Charleston sent rice, Alexandria flour, Baltimore bread and rye, Philadelphia money. Most surprisingly, donations even arrived from London. Since Gage refused to summon the legislature, the members met anyway in Salem and called themselves a "provincial congress." In Philadelphia's Carpenters' Hall the First Continental Congress met to summarize the colonists' grievances and to petition the king.

As the leaves faded and the days drew in, the British officers led a reasonably gay social life with the daughters of both Whigs and Tories. (In that less rigid century it was still possible for political enemies to receive each other socially.) Sam Adams and John Hancock continued to live in Boston, and Colonel Lord Percy was a frequent visitor at the Hancock house, where he quite charmed Hancock's pert fiancée, Dolly Quincy. After an early morning drill on the common, Percy often used to drop in at the Hancock mansion on Beacon Street to enjoy the breakfast company of Dolly and Hancock's Aunt Lydia. The two ladies were much taken with the handsome young earl.

The winter passed—one of the warmest in memory—with the Boston redcoats observing the eighteenth-century army's customary hibernation. On March 5, 1775, Sam Adams and John Hancock were bold enough to hold a Boston Massacre anniversary meeting at the Old South Meeting House. A number of British officers showed up in uniform and were given front-row seats.

The meeting passed off with the usual speeches but without notable incident. At one of the more explosive remarks, some of the British officers called out "Fie! Fie!"—which was understood by the crowd upstairs as "Fire! Fire!" and led to a rapid clearing of the balcony. At the meeting's end, a Boston matron turned on an Irish officer and told him she would like to "ring his nose." But that was all.

Everyone knew that the calm could not last, that spring was bound to bring a change. Some portentous event, as yet unforeseen, was lurking just out of view. And so it turned out on the fateful nineteenth of April at Lexington and Concord.

Although published as a cartoon, this British print reflects the vicious character of Sam Adams' Boston mob. An unfortunate tax collector, who already has been tarred and feathered, is given a dose of boiling tea.

Published after the Port Act had closed Boston, the English satire above shows the city's residents caged and hauled up the Liberty Tree to starve. The fish handed to the prisoners symbolize gifts of food from other towns.

A clash between redcoats and patriots became inevitable when Lord North (right) closed the port of Boston. Despite bitter opposition, North remained prime minister until after the British defeat at Yorktown in 1781.

3

The Redcoats Challenged

News of the engagements at Lexington and Concord spread across New England like a forest fire. Passed on feverishly, the stories grew with each telling. Hearing them, the plowman left his field and the merchant his shop; they picked up their muskets in the furious conviction that British troops had been turned loose on the countryside to burn villages and bayonet old men, women, and children. Rural New Englanders had a mental picture of wanton redcoats pillaging, torturing, murdering. Newspapers proclaiming the "bloody butchery by the British troops" were edged in black, the margins indented with the outlines of coffins.

This feeling was deftly exploited by Dr. Joseph Warren. With both Sam Adams and John Hancock away in Philadelphia, attending the Second Continental Congress, Dr. Warren assumed control of the Committee of Safety set up by the Massachusetts Provincial Congress. He was a more attractive personality than the other two leaders, with none of Sam Adams' fanaticism or Hancock's bombastic vanity. Rather elegant in dress and manner, well-read, with a large medical practice among both the rich and the poor, he was friendly to all—a truly democratic man.

For a long time he had been sacrificing much of his practice to devote time to Whig activities. On the day of Concord and Lexington, Warren had been the only political leader present, and he remained with the pursuing minutemen all the way to Charlestown. Nevertheless, even after that en-

Dr. Joseph Warren, painted here by Copley, abandoned a brilliant medical career to support the colonists' cause. He died in battle soon afterward.

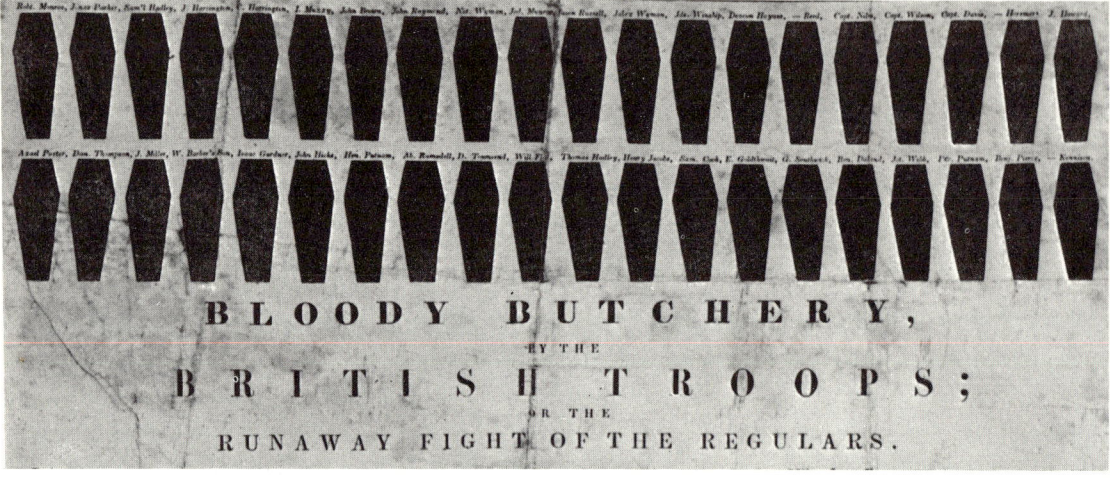

gagement, he did not want complete separation from the mother country. He felt that he and his friends were still transplanted Englishmen defending traditional British rights and freedoms. He was always angered by the taunts of Gage's officers that the colonists would run from the regulars. "Those fellows say we won't fight," Dr. Warren told his friends with unconscious prophecy. "By heavens, I hope I shall die up to my knees in blood."

With the redcoats withdrawn into their Boston citadel, many of the minutemen encamped in the Harvard College Yard in Cambridge to await the next move. From all over New England, militiamen and volunteers began to flock into Cambridge. Sometimes they came in companies, as did Israel Putnam's from Connecticut and Artemas Ward's of Shrewsbury; Ward was soon appointed general of the patchwork army. Sometimes they straggled

Even as the Americans laid siege to Boston, the propaganda war continued. The coffins represent minutemen killed on April 19. It was asked that this poster be shown widely as a reminder of the "bloody butchery."

in singly or in groups, with nothing more than the coats on their backs and the muskets on their shoulders. Some were boys, some old men. Soon there were nearly 15,000 of them. Each man regarded himself as his own general, willing to fight a second Lexington-Concord but certainly not expecting to subject himself to the rigors of military discipline. Hot indignation had brought them there under the elms of Harvard Yard, but a week's rain could easily cool their zeal. Everyone felt as free to leave as he had felt free to come.

Warren and his committee faced a staggering task just in feeding this informal throng. Where were the money, food, and supplies, the ammunition, tents, and clothing? All the complicated organization of an army had to be started from the ground up, and with men who were not even soldiers.

Warren and Ward decided that their best strategy would be to hold the British in Boston, to fortify the neck leading to Roxbury, and to keep a sufficient force in Cambridge to guard against any British counterattack. They well knew how soon the 15,000 men could melt away, and they determined to pick out the most able, enlist them under oath for the remainder of the year, and send the rest home. Eight thousand, double the number of Gage's force, should be enough—they felt—to keep the British tightly bottled up within the Boston peninsula.

John Adams, visiting the fledgling army in Cambridge on his way to the opening of the Second Continental Congress, found "great Confusion and much distress." Yet he noted that the soldiers did not lack "Spirits or Resolution." It was the hope of Adams and Warren to persuade the Congress to make the Provincial army a Continental army with a Continental commander-in-chief.

Meanwhile, behind its water barrier, Boston was ringed with militia in a half-circle from Roxbury to Chelsea. At night, those in the town could see the campfires sparkling like fireflies on the surrounding hills. The Roxbury land approach at the neck was heavily fortified. Both sides agreed, however, to allow the Whigs to leave and the country Tories to enter Boston. In the first few days a torrent of refugees flooded over the neck, by wagon or on foot. The great houses of those who, shortly before, had seemed the most respectable (if not the most popular) members of the community were taken over as barracks by the militiamen.

For a while it seemed a stalemate. The Provincial army was not strong enough to attack the town, while Gage's forces were not large enough to smash their way out. The ships of the Royal Navy protected the harbor and kept Boston's sea routes open; still, the land blockade was soon felt in the overcrowded town as fresh meat and vegetables disappeared.

Between April and June, over 2,700 British troops arrived to reinforce the Boston garrison. An even more emphatic sign that the British government meant business was its dispatch to Boston of three of its most noted generals. On May 25, His Majesty's ship *Cerberus* sailed into Boston harbor carrying Major Generals Henry Clinton, William Howe, and John Burgoyne.

Clinton was a paunchy and colorless little man, competent but lacking in spirit. Howe, a distant cousin of the king and a veteran of the French and Indian Wars, had fought at Louisbourg in 1758, and had led the detachment that scaled the cliffs to Quebec's Plains of Abraham to make Wolfe's victory possible. Large, dark-complexioned, a heavy drinker and gambler, Howe was nevertheless a brave soldier and an able general; being politically a Whig, however, he had little taste for fighting the Americans.

"Gentleman Johnny" Burgoyne was the most dashing of the three. A rarity among generals of his day, he believed in treating his soldiers as human beings, and they responded with their devotion. As gracefully dashing as his nickname, he moved easily in London society, and in fact had written for the stage there. "What!" he had exclaimed on his first shipboard glimpse of the beleaguered town, "Ten thousand peasants keep five thousand King's troops shut up? Well, let *us* get in, and we'll soon find elbowroom!"

Boston's Tories lined the Long Wharf that stretched almost half a mile into the harbor, cheering and waving their handkerchiefs as the generals landed. There was more cheering and applauding as the three made their way over the cobbled streets to pay their respects to Gage at Province House.

In the interval between Lexington and Concord and the arrival of the generals, Gage had concentrated on strengthening the Boston defenses. Two high points of land just outside

These water colors of Boston were done by an English naval officer in 1764. At top is the narrow neck leading to Roxbury; Dorchester Heights is in the background. In the painting at right, across the inlet in the foreground and nearly obscured by ships, is the Long Wharf. The Old North Church is at center; beyond it is Charlestown peninsula.

BOTH: BOSTONIAN SOCIETY

Boston dominated both the town and the harbor: Bunker Hill in Charlestown, to the north; and Dorchester Heights, in a part of Roxbury that is now South Boston, to the south. Admiral Samuel Graves, an otherwise incompetent officer, wisely pointed out to Gage that if these points were seized and fortified by the enemy and armed with cannon, Boston and the warships in its harbor would be doomed.

The admiral was greatly concerned for the safety of the sixty-four-gun *Somerset,* anchored off Charlestown.

On April 19 a detachment of engineers under Captain John Montresor had constructed a small earthwork on top of Bunker Hill. Now, at Copp's Hill in Boston, Admiral Graves ordered his sailors to work building a second earthwork and fortifying it with heavy cannon. He suggested that Gage burn the towns of Roxbury and Charlestown as a safety measure, occupy Dorchester Heights, and expand the Bunker Hill defenses. But Gage was not willing to risk his forces in the hostile region beyond the neck, and he even recalled the detachment sta-

tioned at the Bunker Hill earthwork.

General Clinton was much vexed by Gage's lack of initiative. His trained military eye saw at once the strategic importance of the two heights. Preparations to seize them were begun. Already the rebellious Americans were throwing up earthworks in Roxbury and Cambridge. Inaction can be the death of armies, and the British generals decided it was time for their reinforced army to move. They planned to send out two expeditions, one to cross over Boston Neck and seize Dorchester Heights, the other to oc-

The British 24-pound cannon of the Copp's Hill battery in Boston were about a half-mile from the Breed's Hill redoubt (center background). This sketch, made shortly after the battle, shows the British camps and, at left center, Montresor's reinforced earthwork perched on the top of Bunker Hill.

cupy Bunker Hill and prepare for an attack on Cambridge. The date set for the move was June 18.

In Cambridge, General Ward learned of the British plans almost by chance when a New Hampshire visitor to Boston managed to sneak away with the news that the redcoats were preparing advances on Dorchester and Cambridge. Ward and his officers pondered what action to take.

Despite desertions, quarrels about rank, doubts of Rhode Islanders about Vermonters and vice versa, the Provincial army was going about its elementary drills and assuming some sort of form. Its remaining volunteers began to feel like soldiers. Luckily, food was not yet scarce, although almost everything else was. On June 15 the Committee of Safety met in Cambridge's Hastings house and decided that ". . . it appears of Importance to the Safety of this Colony, that possession of the Hill, called Bunker's Hill, in Charlestown, be securely kept and defended; and also some one hill or hills on Dorchester Neck be likewise Secured." The committee urged that militiamen be ready to march "on the shortest notice, completely equipped, having thirty rounds of cartridges per man."

Theoretically, General Ward now

Henry Clinton, who was an officer at thirteen, became commander-in-chief in North America three years after arriving in Boston.
COLLECTION OF VINTON FREEDLEY

controlled 7,500 men—1,000 more than the British in Boston—but actually there were no more than 5,000 fit for duty, and many of these lacked muskets and ammunition.

On June 16 Colonel William Prescott was ordered to proceed to Bunker Hill and throw up fortifications there. Israel Putnam, a burly, impetuous Indian-fighter known to everyone as Old Put, took it upon himself to visit the Boston Neck fortifications and see what John Thomas, commanding the volunteers there, could do about seizing Dorchester Heights. Thomas had to admit he could do nothing at all, since in a month he had seen the force he commanded dwindle from 6,000 to 2,500. Although reinforced by a detachment of Rhode Islanders under the able Nathanael Greene, Thomas felt he had all he could cope

Disappointed at being sent to Boston, John Burgoyne spent much of his time seeking a more important post in America. In 1777 he planned and commanded the Saratoga campaign, which ended in disaster for the British.

Recruiting sergeants, like the one in this 1779 print, were forced to collect men off England's streets to fill the thin ranks of the British army. One official doubted that there would be enough enlistments "unless it rains men in red coats...."

with in constructing breastworks and defenses in Roxbury.

Even when it was decided to occupy Bunker Hill, Ward, cautious by nature, arranged to keep the bulk of his army in Cambridge. This meant that the force which the general was about to send to Charlestown would march off with too few men and no plans for their later support; further, the men were sadly short of food and water, not to mention artillery and ammunition. Yet Ward must have realized that the British would react at once to his challenge.

Whatever the weaknesses of the Bunker Hill task force, however, it could not have had a better leader than Prescott. As a boy of nineteen he had so distinguished himself in 1745 at the attack on Louisbourg under Sir William Pepperrell that he had been offered a King's commission. He had preferred to go back to farming, but in 1774 Pepperrell's minutemen unanimously elected him their colonel. A tall, commanding figure, who wore his blue-coated uniform as if it were part of him, Prescott's quiet presence fortified and reassured his men.

In the late afternoon of June 16 the Bunker Hill force gathered under the great elms on Cambridge Common. About nine hundred men assembled in the fading light. Some of the officers, like Colonel Prescott, wore blue uniforms and three-cornered hats. The enlisted men wore their own rustic clothes—knee breeches, long stockings, cowhide shoes, and round, large-crowned hats with broad brims. Their homespun coats were dyed "with colors as various as the barks of oak, sumach and other trees of our hills and swamps could make them," and there seemed to be almost as many types of weapons as there were numbers of men.

The force consisted of three Massachusetts regiments—some 300 men belonging to Prescott, 200 under Colonel Ebenezer Bridge, and 350 of Frye's regiment commanded by Dr. (now Lieutenant Colonel) James Brickett, plus the forty-nine men and four fieldpieces of Captain Samuel Gridley's Massachusetts artillery company.

The air was golden-mellow under the shadowing elms of the common, the western sky red with a sunset that promised a fair day to come. The Reverend Dr. Samuel Langdon, who besides being a Congregational minister was also president of Harvard College, stepped before the soldiers in his academic gown. They formed a circle around him as he prayed with stout Whig fervor for the success of the expedition.

Then they marched away in the gathering darkness under a slate-blue sky with the first faint stars blinking at them. Colonel Prescott, a tan smock slung over his arm, led the way, followed by two sergeants carrying dark lanterns "open in the rear." Beside Prescott marched Colonel Richard Gridley, father of Samuel and one of the few Americans to hold a King's commission. Thirty years before, Gridley had taken part in the assault on Louisbourg; in 1758 he fought in the second campaign against the great French fortress, and he had witnessed Wolfe's death at Quebec. The Provincial Congress was delighted to have him serve as chief engineer and chief of artillery of its new army. Unfortunately, Gridley was now an old man.

Prescott led his men due east along the dust-thick road that led through the open country beyond the buildings in the Harvard Yard. None of the soldiers trudging through the dust swirls knew as yet where he was headed.

A half mile beyond Cambridge they crossed Pillon Bridge over Willis Creek. Just beyond lay Lechmere's Point where Colonel Smith's redcoats had landed two months before to begin their fateful march to Lexington. From the bridge the men could see the lights of Boston strung like beads over the invisible hills. As Prescott reached the Charlestown road he found two hundred men of Old Put's Connecticut regiment waiting in the shadows for him. They swung in behind the Massachusetts columns under the com-

Artemas Ward, whose cautious manner irked some of his more energetic officers, had served with General James Abercrombie in the latter's ill-starred attack on Fort Ticonderoga during the French Wars.

mand of slim and vigorous young Captain Thomas Knowlton.

Another half mile and they reached Charlestown Common, following in reverse Paul Revere's midnight route through the marshlands and past the rusty cage that held the Negro Mark's bones. They reached the crossway, where the left road ran to Medford. The lanterns flickered, and Colonel Prescott turned right toward Charlestown Neck and Bunker Hill. Then the men in the ranks knew at last where they were headed.

About a hundred yards past the neck, Prescott halted his columns to hold a conference with his officers. Just what happened at that conference and who was present is still something of a mystery, and the matter has been argued about by historians ever since.

A Roxbury man named Samuel Gray was told, he wrote afterward in a letter to a friend, that Richard Gridley and "two generals went on to the hill at night and reconnoitered the ground." Prescott was one of the "generals," and it seems most likely that the other was the combative Putnam. Some historians believe that Gridley simply wanted to refortify Montresor's Bunker Hill earthwork and that it was Old Put who held out for a lower eminence closer to the British.

Bunker Hill, oval in shape, three hundred yards long and 110 feet high, ran down the center of the mile-long Charlestown peninsula. Beyond it, closer to Boston and facing the Charles River, was a less conspicuous height of land known variously as Charlestown or Breed's Hill. On one side of Breed's Hill lay the now abandoned village of Charlestown; in front of the hill, opposite Boston, were broad meadows sloping down to the water's edge, the pastures marked off by stone walls or rail fences. No farmer had dared to cut the hay that spring, and the grass was waist-high. On the Mystic River side of Breed's were swampy ground, some brick kilns, and a thirty-five-foot mound known as Morton's Hill.

Prescott and his little staff huddling in the darkness finally decided to fortify Breed's Hill. Whether Prescott misunderstood his instructions or whether he was carried away by Old Put's belligerent enthusiasm, Breed's Hill was his decision—and it was the wrong one. If the crest of Bunker Hill had been fortified with cannon, Prescott could have covered all the approaches to the Charlestown peninsula while at the same time remaining safely out of range of the Copp's Hill fort and the guns of the British fleet. Instead, the Americans were to make their challenge on the much less defensible lower level.

While the commanders talked, the men in the ranks grew restless. Finally, the word came to move forward. Captain John Nutting and sixty men were sent to scout out abandoned Charlestown. The remainder moved on to occupy Breed's Hill.

Colonel Gridley did not think much

This rare 1767 view of Harvard College, the first institution of higher learning in the colonies, was engraved by Paul Revere. Each of these buildings, including the chapel at far left, was used to quarter colonial troops during the siege of Boston.

of the position, but he staked out his fortifications as best he could in the dark—a box-shaped fort (called a redoubt) about forty-five yards on each side with a clear field of fire across the length and breadth of the hill's forward slope. The men set to with pick and shovel. Farmers for the most part, used to such tools, they worked swiftly, quietly, and efficiently.

It was a warm, still night, with just enough light in the bluish sky for the diggers to glimpse the outlines of the British ships anchored offshore in the Charles—the *Glasgow* with twenty-four guns, the *Lively* with twenty, the armed transport *Symmetry* with eighteen, and the sloop *Falcon* with sixteen. As the men began their digging, they could hear the Boston clocks across the water tolling midnight and the "All's well!" of the ships' sentries.

In spite of the skill of the men, there was inevitably an occasional clink of a pick against a stone that would make Prescott catch his breath. Twice he crept down to the water's edge to listen for sounds of British activity; nothing broke the silence across the bay but the bells marking the quarter-

hours and the muffled responses of the sentries.

The commander moved up and down the lines among his sweat-stained men, encouraging them with a whispered word here and a pat on the shoulder there. They needed encouraging, for they had not slept in twenty-four hours and had eaten nothing since afternoon. A few became discouraged and drifted away in the direction of the neck, among them old Gridley. The rest, now beginning to suffer severely from thirst, kept to their digging. As the blackness in the east sifted into gray and the stars began to fade, the crude redoubt was finished. Prescott sent for Nutting and his men in Charlestown and assembled all his forces within the raw clay rectangle.

In spite of the silence across the Charles, the British had become aware of the night's activities on the peninsula. Some of the sentinels aboard the ships had heard the diggers, but they had not bothered to make a report. General Clinton had been out on a night patrol and had either heard or seen the rebels. At once he routed out Gage, Howe, and Burgoyne at Prov-

These figures appeared in a British drill manual which was adopted by the Massachusetts militia in 1772. From left to right they show the new recruit how to fix his bayonet, charge, prime and load, fire, and rest his musket.

WINDHAM, *A Plan of Discipline,* 1759

ince House, urging them to launch a two-pronged landing attack "at day brake." Howe was agreeable, but Gage finally persuaded the others to wait until after daylight so that they could then see better just what the provincials were up to.

Boston and Charlestown and their hills emerged slowly from the shadows, a few shreds of mist drifted across the placid water, and below Breed's Hill the meadowlarks began to sing in the tall grass. The all-too-clear morning light showed Prescott what a fearful mistake he had made in concentrating his forces on such a low, unprotected hill.

All the British needed to do was ferry troops across the basin to the peninsula and then, safely out of musket range, march them along the bank of either the Charles or the Mystic until they reached the Charlestown Neck. By fortifying this they could bottle up the provincials and starve them out. It was a victory that could be had without firing a shot. Even the lowliest privates could see the threatening danger, and some of them began to mutter about treachery.

By 4 A.M. the landscape had brightened enough for the lookout on the *Lively* to spot the fresh earthwork on Breed's Hill. He notified Captain Thomas Bishop, who at once warped his ship around to bring her guns to bear on the redoubt. Still smarting from a recent court-martial for neglect of duty, Captain Bishop wasted no time in giving the order to fire. The successive blasts shook Boston's houses and waked the sleeping town. Drummers were soon beating the call to arms, and redcoats poured from their quarters. A boat was lowered from the *Lively,* and its crew pulled hard across the basin toward Boston.

Then for some reason Admiral Graves ordered a let-up in the firing. Prescott used the respite to set his men building a protective breastwork from the redoubt straight down the hill toward the Mystic. But before the diggers had really started, the guns of

COLLECTION OF HAROLD L. PETERSON

The fanciful engraving of an American rifleman (right) was made in Germany about 1775. It was based on a sketch by a Bavarian officer who had served with the British. Few accurate contemporary pictures of American Revolutionary War uniforms exist, although the dress of the colonial artillery crew (left) is depicted faithfully. It was etched on a powder horn.

the whole fleet opened up. From water level the cannon could not be elevated high enough to do much damage to the redoubt, but at first the noise and the smoke struck fear in the green provincials. Suddenly there was blood on the grass, and the diggers peered down to see the remains of Asa Pollard of Bridge's regiment sprawled in the dirt, his head severed by a cannon ball. The others dropped their tools and gathered around the body. Prescott kept ordering them back to work, but they continued to stand there in mute dismay. A clergyman stepped forward and offered to perform the burial service. Even as he was praying, more men began to slip away toward the safety of the neck.

By now the sun was well up in the serene and cloudless sky, promising a shimmeringly hot day. Prescott drove his men at their digging, giving them no time to brood. Minus hat and wig, his bald head glistening, he walked with slow deliberation along the parapet, impervious to British shot. He had taken off his blue tunic and replaced it with his linen smock. As he chatted with his soldiers, his air of confidence seemed undiminished. A lucky shot from one of the ships had destroyed the two hogsheads of water in the redoubt, and the men's thirst galled them. "We began to be almost beat out," a man recalled, "being tired by our Labour and having no sleep the night before, but little victuals, no Drink but Rum."

Meanwhile, at Province House, Gage prolonged his breakfast conference with his three generals. Clinton still insisted that troops should be embarked at once, and no time lost, before Prescott could complete his fortifications. He wanted the main force under Howe to attack the redoubt from the front while he himself, with five hundred troops, would go up the Mystic to seize the rebel rear. Although a milldam blocked a direct landing on the neck from the Charles River side, Admiral Graves could easily bring up floating batteries and bar the Americans from crossing there—in effect, cutting off the Breed's Hill force from both reinforcements and escape.

To Howe and Burgoyne, Clinton's plan seemed unnecessarily complicated merely to drive a crowd of ragamuffins out of their wretched earthworks. The generals had the disdain of the professional for the amateur, of the English gentleman for the colonial rustic that was characteristic of so many British officers. Howe was not even willing to call the prospective engagement a fight. The provincials, he announced contemptuously, were to be "removed" from the redoubt. Breed's Hill was "open and of easy assent and in short would be easily carried."

The British then began their preparation for the assault with a leisurely thoroughness that gave Prescott the much-needed time to reinforce his lines toward the Mystic, where he felt any attack would probably be made.

This banner was carried by the British 5th regiment, which took part in Howe's assault on Breed's Hill. The 5th later fought in the New York and Pennsylvania campaigns.

Since this action was to be technically an expedition, the redcoats were ordered to take full regulation field packs. This meant that for a journey of a few hundred yards on one of the hottest days of the year they would have to carry knapsacks with blankets as well as all their other equipment and three days' cooked rations—in all about 125 pounds on their backs as they attacked.

Orders poured out of Province House: ten companies of grenadiers and ten of light infantry, plus the 5th and 38th regiments, to proceed to Long Wharf for embarkation; the 43rd and 52nd regiments and the rest of the grenadiers and light infantry to leave from the North Battery wharf. These two assault waves numbered about 1,550 men. A reserve detachment—the 47th regiment, part of the 63rd, and the 1st and 2nd battalions of marines—was to stand by at the North Battery.

While the British troops were gathering, Prescott's men were using stone walls and rail fences to extend the breastwork. The nine- and twelve-pounders of the warships in the basin continued to fire with more noise than damage. By this time the provincials were becoming sufficiently "cannon-wise" to duck at the first flash of the muzzles and watch the iron balls—even those of the twenty-four-pounders in the Copp's Hill battery—arch over their heads harmlessly.

Captain Samuel Gridley managed to get four guns up to the redoubt, and his artillerists opened fire on Boston. But after half a dozen shots in which they missed their targets by a sizable margin and merely hit a fence and a house, they quit in discouragement and began to look for some way of pulling out.

There were gaps in the ranks as more of Prescott's men, by two's and

Prescott's men worked throughout the night to erect defenses atop Breed's Hill. Although the meager American force desperately needed artillery, most of the gunners fled the peninsula before the British attack.

three's now, slipped away to the Cambridge mainland. Even those who stayed kept looking toward the neck and grumbling about the absence of the expected relief. Prescott knew that they were not going to be relieved at all, but he finally sent Major John Brooks to Cambridge to ask General Ward for reinforcements. (As Gridley flatly refused to give him one of his artillery horses, Brooks had to go on foot.) At the neck, where the brisk fire from the warships' guns was finding the range, Brooks met Old Put bustling along. Putnam was everywhere that morning, delivering his orders himself since he had no staff.

The ailing Ward, who had been hesitant about the Bunker Hill move from the beginning, at first refused to consider sending any more men there at all. Anybody could see that the British were making ready to strike, but where they might strike was another matter. Suppose they should make a feint at Charlestown and then advance instead on Cambridge? What would happen to all the painfully collected provincial stores and ammunition if there were no troops left to protect them?

The Committee of Safety meeting in the Hastings house—without Dr. Warren, who was for the moment laid low with a bad headache—overruled their general. Aid, they felt, must be sent at once to Prescott. They ordered out Reed's regiment along with the rest of John Stark's New Hampshire troops. Each man was issued two flints, a gill of powder, and a pound of lead cut from the organ of a Cambridge church. This force set out at just about the time that barges of redcoats were shoving off from Boston.

During that explosive morning everyone in Boston whose feet would carry him made his way to the north side of the town. Roofs and garrets were crowded with spectators. Rarely has a battle had such a panoramic view and so many onlookers. General Gage came down to the waterfront with Abijah Willard, the Tory brother of Prescott's wife, and inspected the redoubt with his spyglass. Willard pointed out the commanding figure on the parapet as his brother-in-law.

"Will he fight?" Gage asked him.

"I cannot answer for his men," Willard told the general, "but Prescott will fight you to the gates of hell."

The slam and crash of the ships' guns reverberated as far away as Braintree, where on Penn's Hill Abigail Adams watched the far-off smoke as she held the hand of a little boy who would one day be the sixth president of the United States. To the watchers on the Boston rooftops it was like a pageant. Yet when one of the little antlike figures on the earthworks opposite dropped down, he was really dead. Even as the people on the roofs watched, a man standing next to Colonel Prescott was torn apart by a chance shot. Each time the big guns belched their orange flashes, the brown figures on Breed's Hill scurried down like insects to let the cannon balls sail over. Black coils of smoke twisted and spread over the placid water. The meadow grass below the redoubt seemed a green sea, with here and there a furrow cut by a shell.

The stage for the pageant was long set. Then, at half-past one, the curtain rose. Twenty-eight barges of redcoats left the shelter of the Boston wharves and headed across the channel to Morton's Point on Charlestown peninsula.

Those who saw that flotilla never forgot the cruel, precise beauty of it. Two parallel lines of fourteen boats moved in clockwork order across the water, white oars flashing in perfect cadence. In each of the leading barges six polished brass six-pounders flashed back the sunshine. The soldiers in the following barges sat at attention, the gilded insignia of their peaked helmets glittering, their bayonets coldly bright. Their red tunics were faced with blue or white or yellow and crossed by white pipe-clayed belts. The stiff stocks at their necks, the queued and powdered hair curled at the sides, gave their faces beneath the helmets the unbending expression of marionettes.

So the doomed files passed in their moment of scarlet and silver and gold, in the pageantry of their century that had tried to make war as formal and precise as a minuet.

4

Bunker Hill

One by one the barges ground ashore at Morton's Point. The redcoats, with haversacks and muskets, splashed through the shallows and up the beach. Then the barges returned to Boston for a second load, this time bringing back the Royal Regiment of Artillery and General Howe. The landing, well protected by the guns of the Royal Navy, was made without opposition. A total of 1,550 British troops arrived in the first two waves.

From the shore Howe observed Stark's and Reed's regiments on the crest of Bunker Hill, and as he watched he noticed several detachments hurry downhill and move into positions along the flat land just above the Mystic River. Howe saw at once that these newcomers would block any chance he might have had to move his troops along the Mystic and seal off the provincials from the rear.

About four hundred yards from the rough breastwork, Howe lined up four companies of his light infantry under the protection of a small bank. Then, after he had formed up his other

Thomas Gage had nearly twenty years of military experience in the colonies before the Revolution. In Copley's portrait he points to what is probably an event in the French Wars, during which he served with Braddock and in the Montreal campaign.

Three of the American officers at Breed's Hill stand resolutely beneath the Massachusetts Pine Tree flag in this detail from John Trumbull's painting of the battle. William Prescott (far right) commanded the colonial force and led the defenses in the redoubt. Next to him stands Andrew McClary, who was killed in the retreat; Thomas Knowlton, in the white shirt, repulsed the British attack on the rail fence.

troops and pushed three lines of infantry to the top of Morton's Hill, he sent back to Gage to ask for reinforcements. In the interval the men broke ranks, unfastened their knapsacks, took off their helmets, and—securely out of rebel range—sat down in the grass to eat their dinner.

As he had watched the redcoats pile ashore, Prescott realized that the most vulnerable spot in his lines was the gap where the breastwork ended in swampy ground short of the Mystic. In the breathing space now given him, he sent Captain Knowlton and his two hundred Connecticut men to close the gap. He also sent Captain Gridley with his fieldpieces, but as soon as Gridley and his disheartened artillerists were out of sight of the redoubt, they changed direction and headed for the neck. Old Put stopped them near Bunker Hill. Gridley's men insisted they were out of ammunition, but the suspicious Putnam inspected the ammunition chests, found them full, and angrily ordered the guns back to the firing line. When he turned his back, however, the gunners abandoned their pieces and fled the peninsula.

Captain Knowlton was made of sterner stuff. Determined, if somewhat uncertain of his orders, he moved his company back of the swamp some six hundred feet behind the breastwork to a stone wall topped by fence railings that marked an old ditch. The wall ran parallel to the breastwork and extended two hundred yards to the Mystic. His men tore down another rail fence and set it up just ahead of their own. The space between they filled with grass and brush. There was still a gap between the rail fence and the breastwork, a gap only partially taken up by the swamp. Here Knowlton dug three small V-shaped trenches called flèches.

When John Stark, standing atop Bunker Hill, saw how much space Knowlton was attempting to hold with his few men, he at once led his own force down the hill on the double to reinforce them. Stark paused a moment to give his men "a short but animated address," to which the troops answered with three cheers. They joined Knowlton just about the time that General Howe was landing with the second load of troops.

Also at this time Captain Samuel Trevett showed up with two fieldpieces from Cambridge, which he had brought safely through the British fire at the neck. These two guns, placed behind the rail fence, provided the only effective American artillery fire of the day. A British officer remarked that the cannon were "very advantageously planted," and added that the Yankee gunners served them "with the greatest vigor." Trevett's guns and Stark's unit were the last important reinforcements the defenders of Breed's Hill would receive.

Stark, walking along the line of rail fence, found that it ended at the riverbank. There the bank dropped sharply eight or nine feet to a narrow beach, a perfectly shielded route for the redcoats to march along and outflank Prescott's whole army. At once Stark ordered "his boys" to pile up stones and make a solid wall on the beach right down to the water's edge. Behind this wall he posted a triple row of marksmen.

Shortly after the alarm sounded in Cambridge, Dr. Warren started out for Charlestown. He galloped across the neck, disregarding the pounding Royal Navy cannonade, and made his way up Bunker Hill. The Provincial Congress had just elected him a major general, and Old Put soon came over and asked the new commander for orders. Warren said he had come to fight as a volunteer in the ranks, not as a general. When he reached the redoubt, Prescott, too, offered him the command, but Warren insisted that since he had not yet officially received his commission, he had no command. He borrowed a musket and took his place in the line.

Seth Pomeroy, a seventy-year-old veteran of the French Wars, had also been made a general by the Congress. He tramped across the neck and up to Breed's Hill with the musket he had carried thirty years before at the siege of Louisbourg. Like Warren he insisted on fighting as a volunteer and joined Stark's men by the fence.

As the climax of the afternoon approached, there were others who showed themselves less courageous. Behind the American lines the confusion was worse than the cannonading. Out of the nine regiments originally dispatched from Cambridge, only five of varying strength arrived at Breed's Hill. Some regiments got lost, some were warned away by the thunder of the guns across the neck, some stopped short at Bunker Hill.

While waiting for his reserves, and to protect himself from snipers and any surprise attack, Howe ordered Admiral Graves to set fire to Charlestown. The admiral proceeded to bombard the village with red-hot cannon balls, and soon whole rows of buildings burst into flames.

The cannonading from the ships increased in tempo as the barges with Howe's reserve detachment landed between Morton's Point and burning Charlestown. The detachment consisted of 700 men—the remaining light infantry and grenadiers, the 47th regiment, and a battalion of marines. Howe now had 2,250 infantrymen under his command, plus artillery. He divided his force into two wings, taking over the right wing to make the major attack, and leaving the left wing to his second-in-command, Brigadier General Sir Robert Pigot.

At three o'clock the British drums beat the call to arms. Howe arranged his men in three lines, the classic British order of attack. The light infantry was in front, the grenadiers in the second line, and the men of the 5th and 52nd regiments in the rear. To the waiting Americans it looked as if the English general were staging a direct frontal assault.

But Howe, though contemptuous of

Colonial troops scramble into position behind the Breed's Hill breastwork moments before the first British charge. Hastily built "under a very warm fire from the enemy's artillery," the breastwork extended from the redoubt about 165 feet toward the Mystic to protect the Americans' exposed left flank.

EMMET COLLECTION, N.Y. PUBLIC LIBRARY

An English officer's water color shows Charlestown almost completely enveloped by fire as the Glasgow *(left) and the* Symmetry *rake the American positions. At right, redcoats row ashore to attack Breed's Hill, visible directly above the flaming town.*

the un-uniformed provincials, was no fool. He first moved his light infantry, the key to his battle plan, off to the right and formed them up on the beach. This force was to slip along the Mystic shore, turn the Americans' flank, and attack them from the rear. Then his two remaining lines, led by the grenadiers, would charge with bayonets up the lower slope of Breed's Hill toward the breastwork and the rail fence. At the same time Pigot's men were to come in from the Charles River side, skirt Charlestown, and attack the redoubt itself.

To the provincials, listening to the long roll of the drums, the scarlet ranks of infantry forming their precise lines were an ominous sight. These soldiers with their peaked helmets and glittering bayonets formed the world's most formidable fighting machine. In open combat they were unequaled, as they had proved from Flanders to Quebec.

Few records are left of how the parched and weary amateur soldiers felt watching them, but the massed bayonets must have been particularly dismaying to those who had none. Private Peter Brown had the feeling that "they advanced towards us in order to swallow us up." Prescott was manning the redoubt and the breastwork with his own men, along with bits and pieces of several other regiments, all of them composed of Massachusetts troops. The rail fence was held by Knowlton's Connecticut troops, Reed's New Hampshire men,

and some of Stark's. Stark himself and the rest of his men guarded the wall by the beach. Three companies protected the Charlestown flank.

Just before the signal for the attack, Howe addressed his men in the formal eighteenth-century manner, telling them he was sure they would "behave like Englishmen, and as becometh good soldiers." He would not ask one of them "to go a step further than where I go myself at your head." It was a promise he kept.

Before moving his infantry, he sent his artillery forward to open fire on the redoubt, the breastwork, and the fence. Unfortunately for him, his brass six-pounders had been supplied with twelve-pound shot, and the distance was too great for grapeshot to

Covered by naval guns, unwavering ranks of British troops march toward Breed's Hill. In the 1880's five foreign artists executed a huge cyclorama of the battle. The 240-foot-long painting was exhibited in Boston and enjoyed brief popularity. A set of photographs of it were taken (of which this is one); then it disappeared without a trace.

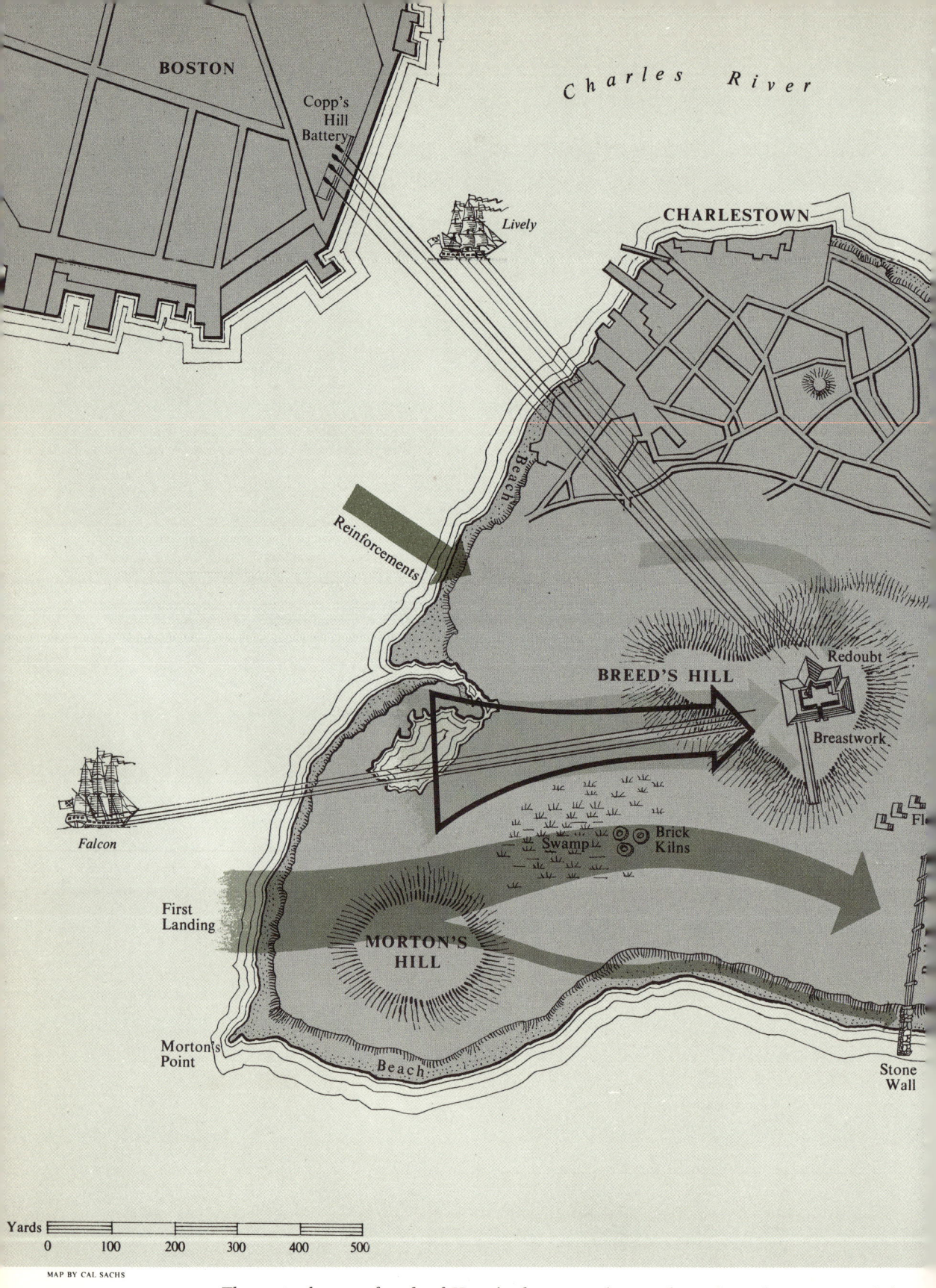

The main thrusts of each of Howe's three attacks are shown here, beginning with his double-pronged strike against the rail fence and the stone wall. Repelled with severe losses, he then launched a frontal assault, which failed dismally, against the redoubt

and the breastwork. In the third and decisive charge, late in the afternoon, Pitcairn's marines (curving around the American right flank) and the combined forces of Clinton and Pigot took the weakened redoubt, while Howe's troops carried the breastwork.

be effective. There was further difficulty when the guns bogged down in the soggy ground. (Gage's chief of artillery was later roundly criticized for the ammunition mix-up. An officer sarcastically commented that if the artillery colonel had spent more time attending to his business and less time "dallying with the schoolmaster's daughters" in Boston, things might have been different.)

While the artillerists tugged at their cannon, the grenadiers and the infantry in the line behind them began their direct advance, each man still burdened by his 125-pound pack. Howe felt that they would not need to stop and fire. The cold steel of the bayonet would be enough.

Down Morton's Hill the red lines moved, steady and exact, in time to the beat of the drums, across the flatland, and up the lower slope of Breed's Hill. Three hundred abreast they marched, as if they were on parade. It was a slow and ponderous advance, hindered by the long pasture grass, interrupted by walls and fences, dislocated by swamps, and even broken briefly by the brick kilns. From time to time the two lines stopped to let the artillery come up.

From the hills and roofs of Boston the slowness of the advance, magnified as it was by the distance, was breath-catching. For those watchers unaccustomed to violence, such a display gave the curious sense of living in a dream. Against the background of what might have been an indolent summer day, flame belched from the Copp's Hill battery and the guns of the fleet; Charlestown blazed, buildings crashing with showers of sparks and tongues of flame licking up the church spires. Against the green meadow the waving red lines moved relentlessly; the smoke from the burning town almost obscured the small brown figures behind the redoubt and the breastwork.

Yet, for the onlookers, those dots of brown, those lines of scarlet, were men like themselves who in the next few minutes might be dead. And it gripped the watchers' hearts to realize that this grand game under the hot afternoon sun was a game that men were playing with their lives.

As the red wave of infantry lapped against the foot of Breed's Hill, the Royal Navy gunners held their fire. The provincials waited behind their rough earthworks and flimsy fences with flintlocks cocked. They could now see the numbered regimental badges of the grenadiers and even the coat buttons. There were no other

William Howe resigned his post in America less than three years after the battle at Breed's Hill, charging that the home government no longer supported him. In this English print, Howe wears the Order of the Bath, awarded for his 1776 victory at Long Island.

A British drummer boy

sounds but the ominous beat of the drums and the heavy tread of advancing feet.

American officers paced back and forth behind their troops, urging them to fire slowly, aim low, and concentrate on the British officers. Prescott is said to have passed the word along to his waiting men, "Don't fire until you see the whites of their eyes!" Perhaps he did, for the remark had become almost a military commonplace since it had first been made thirty years before by Prince Charles of Prussia at the Battle of Jägerndorf. In any case, they held their fire.

The light infantry that had moved off to the beach was able to advance more rapidly along the packed sand. Eleven companies were there, marching in columns of fours: the Royal Welch Fusiliers in the lead, followed by a company of the King's Own. Their orders were not to stop to fire but to take the wall with the bayonet.

Stark's men let them come on until they were only fifty feet away and preparing to charge home. Suddenly a row of muskets appeared, a nasal New England voice commanded "Fire!" and the wall vanished behind a blaze of flame and curling black smoke. The blast ripped the ranks of the fusiliers apart, dropping some, scattering the rest. The men of the King's Own pushed their way dauntlessly forward only to be met by another hail of bullets that stopped them in their tracks. Officers bellowed for the men to reform, but even as they stepped over their own dead and wounded, they were cut down.

The bodies piled up on the narrow beach that was like a tunnel into which the Americans poured their shot. Some of the redcoats fell in the sand, others in the water; again and again the front ranks dissolved. Finally, in the face of that withering fire, panic seized the survivors. Even the officers, lashing at the men with their swords, could no longer rally them. They bolted for the rear, leaving behind ninety-six dead. The first and most important part of Howe's plan—to outflank the provincials—had failed.

Now it was the turn of the grenadiers, led by Howe in person as he had promised, in a direct frontal attack on the rail fence. The grenadiers were just clambering over their last obstacle when they heard the volleys and the shouting from the beach. Scattered shots came from a few Americans behind the fence, and the redcoats stopped to return the fire. As they did so the full provincial firepower from behind the barricades hit them with almost the force that struck the Royal Welch.

Howe was unhurt, but his staff lay dead and wounded all around him, and his grenadiers dropped right and left. The British return fire went high and wide. The redcoats bunched in the grass made perfect targets for the farmers steadying their muskets on the fence rails. The line of regulars advancing behind the grenadiers was riddled. Never could their thrusting

A British grenadier officer

bayonets get close enough for the final charge.

As the redcoats dropped in windrows, disorder grew. Even disciplined flesh can stand only so much. Finally, the British turned and fled out of range of the deadly fire.

Pigot's flanking column on the extreme left was also a flat failure. American snipers, hiding behind rocks and trees and dodging between the burning buildings in Charlestown, nearly drove the redcoats to distraction. When Pigot saw what had happened to Howe, he called his men back before they got anywhere near the redoubt.

The Americans cheered and shouted as if victory were already theirs. They had met the terrible regulars and had

In a detail from the cyclorama, Knowlton's men (left background) riddle the grenadiers trying to take the rail fence. The view is from Breed's Hill toward the Mystic River.

overcome them. Prescott knew, however, that the battle was far from won, that the regulars would soon be back. He had few defenders—only 150 now in the redoubt, perhaps another 700 behind the breastwork and the fence.

Old Put climbed up Bunker Hill, where several hundred men were preparing a second line of defense. Though he begged and cursed at them

In Howard Pyle's nineteenth-century painting the second assault wave of grim redcoats, as neatly aligned as toy soldiers, starts up the body-strewn slopes of Breed's Hill.

to go forward and aid Prescott, only a few responded. Other reinforcements were still stalled at the neck by the guns of the warships.

Within fifteen minutes of his bloody repulse, Howe had rallied his men to launch a second attack. This time he combined the thinned ranks of his light infantry and grenadiers to storm the rail fence, while he and Pigot threw the rest of their force against the breastwork and the redoubt. In cadence with the drums, they marched forward in columns to within a hundred yards of the American lines, where they formed their line of battle and moved off with bayonets at the ready.

The provincials let them advance until they were thirty yards away. Then again there came that withering downhill rain of shot. "As we approached," a British officer recalled, "an incessant stream of fire poured from the rebel lines; it seemed a continued sheet of fire for near thirty minutes. Our Light-infantry were served up in Companies against the grass fence, without being able to penetrate—indeed, how could we penetrate? Most of our Grenadiers and Light-infantry, the moment of presenting themselves, lost three-fourths, and many nine-tenths, of their men. Some had only eight or nine men a company left; some only three, four, and five. On the left Pigot was staggered and actually retreated. Observe, our men were not driven back; they actually retreated by orders."

The British lines tangled with each other, broke, and dissolved into individual redcoats running pell-mell downhill to get out of range of the Yankee guns. Howe stood there shocked among the dead and dying. It was, he confessed later, "a Moment I never felt before."

The British wounded who could be gathered up were taken to the boats and ferried to Boston. Howe regrouped his shaken survivors at the bank of the Charles. His remaining officers now begged him to call off the engagement, but the general was stubbornly determined to make one more attempt. He sent over to Clinton, who was responsible for the reserves, to demand still more men.

Clinton dispatched four hundred men of the 63rd regiment and the 2nd marine battalion. He had been watching the engagement from Copp's Hill, and now, as he saw Pigot's men huddled leaderless near the Charlestown shore, it was more than he could bear. He had himself rowed across. Picking up what stragglers and walking wounded he could, he made his way toward the battleground.

The sharp joy of Prescott's men at the second repulse of the regulars was short-lived when they saw the red lines forming for the third time. Although their casualties had been light, the provincials—from redoubt to rail fence—were almost out of powder and bullets. Men shared what they had with their comrades; Prescott located a few cannon cartridges left behind by

The British grenadiers and the light infantry lost a total of nearly 70 per cent of their strength storming the rebel positions on Breed's Hill. This contemporary American engraving erroneously depicts Israel Putnam (on horseback at left) commanding the defensive lines during one of the enemy assaults.

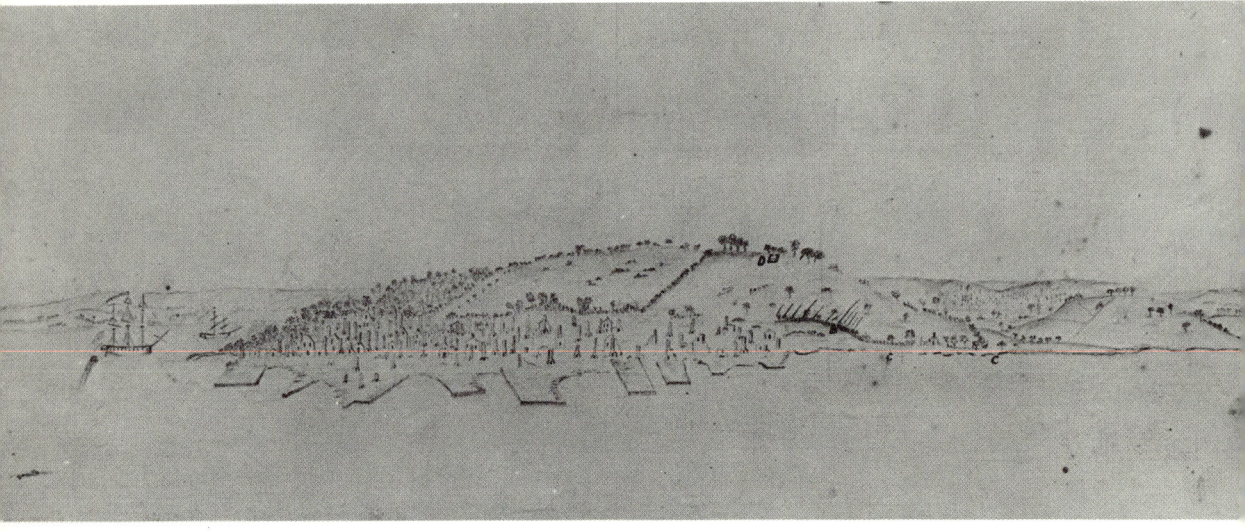

The deliberate British destruction of Charlestown, shown above in a drawing found in General Clinton's papers, infuriated the colonists. In a letter to England a Bostonian declared, "It was a pretty town! but now there is not one house left standing! It is nothing but a heap of ruins." C. W. Peale sketched the Revolutionary War cannon below.

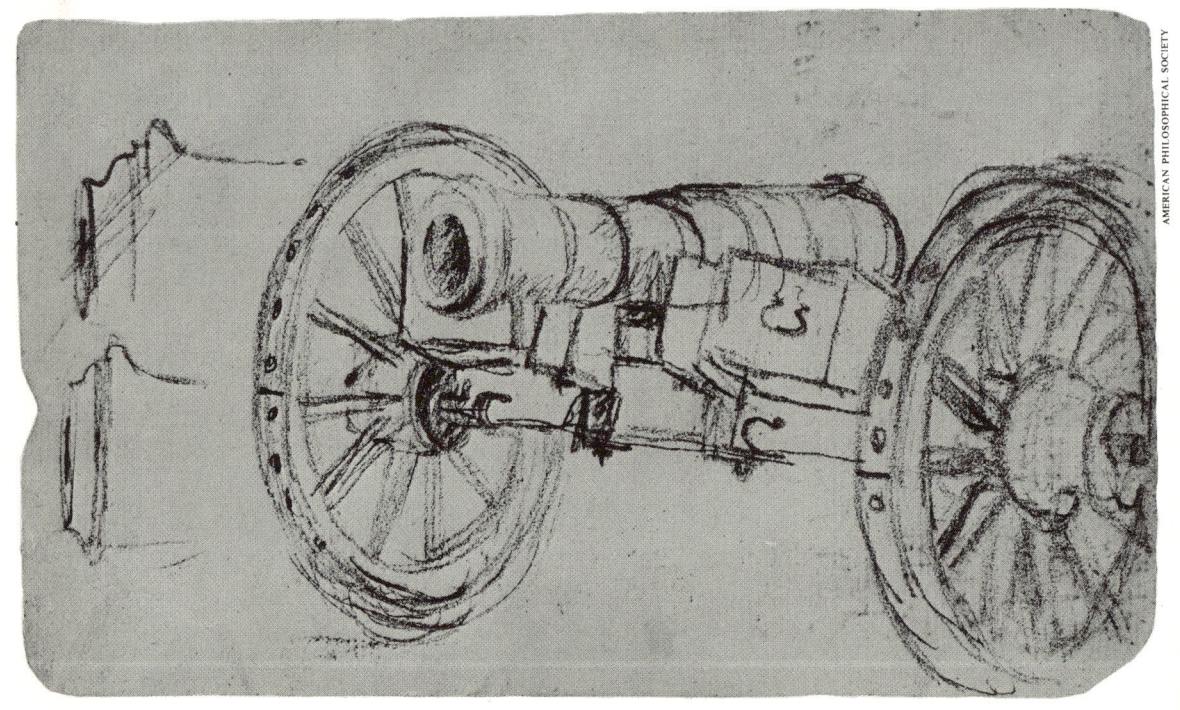

Gridley's gunners, broke them open, and distributed this small stock of powder. Still, the defenders were far short of what was needed to meet another determined assault.

Behind the Yankee lines there was the continuing, confusing mixture of bravery and cowardice. Hundreds still milled about at the neck, taking shelter in hollows, behind rocks, even behind haystacks. A few went resolutely forward to join the fighting. Others as resolutely made their way to the rear. Two youngsters hauled a pitcher of rum and a pail of water all the way across the neck and up to the battle lines on Breed's Hill. They were warmly greeted by the parched defenders, and one of the boys recalled that their "rum and water went very quick."

Hundreds of fresh men wandered aimlessly on the reverse slope of Bunker Hill. Old Put did his profane best to urge them to move down to the redoubt, but without success. "I could not *drive* the dogs," he admitted afterward.

The sun was lowering and the shadows long, as the British formed for their third assault. This time they had brought up artillery with cannon balls that fitted. Howe would lead the attack against the breastwork, Pigot and Clinton against the redoubt. Only a handful of troops were to make a feint at the rail fence. For this final assault, common sense at last won out over military regulations: Howe ordered his men to discard their knapsacks and all other superfluous equipment.

Again the drums echoed their sinister rhythm, and again the redcoats with their flashing bayonets came on over the bloody, trampled grass where their comrades still lay. This time they advanced in open order in long files, each file twelve feet from the next. When a man dropped, the man behind him took his place, stepping over the body as if it were a log. One of the waiting provincials, watching the deadly scarlet files moving toward him, remembered that "they looked too handsome to be fired at; but we had to do it."

As the British artillery opened up, holes gaped in the breastwork, but still there was no break in Prescott's defenses. Still the provincials' rain of fire cut down the advancing redcoats, maddened now by the lust of battle that can overcome fear. "Suddenly," a young lieutenant, Lord Rawdon, wrote, "our men grew impatient, and all crying 'Push on, push on,' advanced with infinite spirit to attack the work with their small arms. As soon as the rebels perceived this, they rose up and poured in so heavy a fire upon us that the oldest officers say they never saw a sharper action. They kept up this fire until we were within ten yards of them. . . . There are few instances of regular troops defending a redoubt till the enemy were in the very ditch of it . . . [yet] I myself saw several pop their heads up and fire even after some of our men were upon the berm. . ."

John Trumbull did this pencil portrait of Israel Putnam. Old Put had nearly been burned alive by Indians during his spectacular career with Rogers' Rangers in the French Wars.

At Pigot's far left the marines were momentarily shattered by fire from the redoubt. Major Pitcairn, unhurt on the retreat from Concord and Lexington, now received a mortal wound while trying to rally his men. Supported by the 47th, the marines recovered their strength and stormed the walls of the redoubt "under a most sore and heavy fire."

Provincials who ran short of bullets fired nails or small pieces of metal they picked up. Others, completely out of ammunition, hurled rocks at the advancing British columns.

For a moment, as the redcoats poised, the battle lay in the balance. A few of the idle companies from Bunker Hill might have swung that balance to the provincials, or a few extra pounds of powder. Prescott thought afterward that one more volley would have pushed the British down the hill. Instead, with the last grains of powder exhausted, the American fire sputtered out "like an old candle." The grenadiers and the marines quickly scrambled over the walls, bayonets thrust forward, with the hoarse, traditional victory shout that could be heard as far as Boston. Within the smoky redoubt, provincials and redcoats fought like wild animals, clubbed muskets against bayonets, stones against swords, even fists against fists.

Prescott saw that the end had come and ordered a retreat. The men jammed at the one narrow exit in the rear. So great was the dust and smoke,

Trumbull's rough sketch for his painting of the Breed's Hill battle shows a Connecticut officer (left) and his Negro servant, Salem Prince. Prince is said to have mortally wounded Major Pitcairn.

EDGAR WILLIAM AND BERNICE CHRYSLER GARBISCH COLLECTION, NATIONAL GALLERY OF ART

In this primitive painting of the battle, shells from the Copp's Hill guns arch over the Charles, as unrealistically neat ranks of redcoats and colonials clash by the beach.

however, that the redcoats on the walls did not dare fire into the wild and groping mass for fear of killing their own men. Most of the provincials at last managed to break free, but somewhere in the smoky tumult Dr. Warren fell with a bullet through his brain. "He died in his best cloaths," a British officer noted. "Every body remembers his fine silk-fringed waistcoat." The resistance at the redoubt was over.

Luckily for the desperate provincials, Stark's men behind the rail fence managed to cover the retreat before they too withdrew. Old Seth Pomeroy stayed until the end, the stock of his Louisbourg musket shattered, backing off so that he could still face the enemy.

Led by Pitcairn's marines, the British flanking column breaks into the redoubt and sends the beaten Americans scurrying for safety. The cannon shown in the redoubt had been withdrawn before the attack began. Charlestown blazes in the background of this scene from the Breed's Hill cyclorama.

Clinton found Howe too dazed to continue, his face blank, his white gaiters red with the blood that smeared the long grass. Leaving a hundred men in the redoubt, the younger general at once organized a pursuit. But the American retreat was, General Burgoyne admitted, "no flight; it was even covered with bravery and military skill." Stark and Knowlton put

up a stubborn rear-guard defense, their men pausing to deliver a withering fire from behind each wall and fence before falling back. The rebels managed to haul away one of Captain Trevett's two guns, the only American artillery piece to be saved.

At the neck the situation was different. Here more than a thousand exhausted men found the remainder of their courage oozing away as they struggled to cross the thirty-five-yard bottleneck while at the same time being raked by the guns of the *Glasgow* and riddled by British musket fire from the rear. By the time the last provincials crossed the neck, they had lost more men there than during the battle. The day's casualties for the Americans were 140 killed, 271 wounded, and 30 captured.

The British losses were staggering— nearly half the redcoats engaged were casualties, including a disproportionate number of officers picked off by Yankee sharpshooters. The dead numbered 226, and 828 were wounded. Although in possession of the Charlestown peninsula, the British had neither the will nor the strength to go farther. "A dear bought victory," Clinton wrote that evening. "Another such would have ruined us."

The hand-to-hand fighting in the redoubt is depicted in Alonzo Chappel's painting of the climax of the battle. Recalling General Burgoyne's boast before the battle, an Englishman wrote, "We have got a little elbow-room, but I think we have paid too dearly for it."

125

5

Boston Besieged

Night came, heavy and overcast, and Charlestown Neck lay empty. The Americans had withdrawn into the shadows of Cambridge, and the cannon of the fleet ceased their fire. On the slopes of Breed's Hill and along the littered beach, stretcher-bearers and surgeons moved through the sultry hours bringing off the wounded, guided in the darkness by moans or sometimes screams.

Back and forth between Morton's Point and Boston's Long Wharf the barges labored with their loads of broken bodies. The lights of the search parties flickered up and down the peninsula, still partially illuminated by the glow and occasional shower of sparks from smoldering Charlestown. At Long Wharf coaches, chariots, chaises, and even wheelbarrows waited to carry away the maimed. The almshouse, the workhouse, and an old factory were taken over for hospitals.

Although more than half the Boston garrison had taken no part in the battle, the spirit had gone out of the whole occupying army. Soon the previously smart redcoats would be appearing on the streets in sloppy uniforms, with soiled gaiters and webbing, unkempt hair, unpolished boots

George Washington, standing at Dorchester Heights in Gilbert Stuart's portrait, took command of the American forces besieging Boston shortly after Breed's Hill. Ironically, Washington and Gage had served together during the French and Indian Wars.

and badges—a sure sign in any army of disintegrating morale. "The loss we have Sustained is greater than we can bear," General Gage wrote from Province House to his friend Lord Barrington in London. "I wish this Cursed place was burned!"

To Gage it seemed that there was nothing left for his penned-up army to do now but quit Boston. Howe felt that there was nothing to do for the moment but stay on. Clinton was more aggressive, and wanted to seize Dorchester Heights before the Americans recovered from their defeat. But Gage could not bear the thought of any more offensive action. He would do no more than strengthen the defenses at Boston Neck and enlarge Montresor's works on Bunker Hill into a solid fort.

It would take a good many years before the Bunker Hill engagement (as it came to be known, incorrectly) would be seen in its true light as one of the decisive battles of the Revolution. Before that bloody afternoon that left British dead strewn along the slopes of Breed's Hill, it might have been possible—even after Concord and Lexington—for the colonists and the mother country to work out some sort of accommodation. But after Bunker Hill, as anger and bitterness raged on both sides, it was no longer possible.

Only gradually, as Americans came to understand the significance of the battle, did Prescott's valiant fight achieve the symbolism of a heroic act. Practically speaking it was a foolish one. Even if Prescott had seized the higher level of Bunker Hill and established himself there, he lacked the heavy cannon necessary to threaten Boston. From a purely military view it will always be a question of which side behaved the more foolishly—the Americans in setting themselves up in an advanced position that could easily have been surrounded, or the British who attacked that position head on.

For the rebels the first reaction to Bunker Hill was the numbness of defeat. They had, after all, lost the battle and been thrown off the hill. Many of them felt great hostility toward Artemas Ward for staying in Cambridge and issuing no orders during the engagement. The men who fought were extremely bitter about the men who did not. Several officers were courtmartialed and dismissed from the service.

Tactically the British had won a victory. But from a larger point of

When Henry Pelham, a Massachusetts Tory, did this map in 1776, British defenses in Boston and Charlestown were checkmated by American artillery positions. The most important of these was at Dorchester Heights, jutting into the harbor at lower left. Cambridge, the rebel headquarters, is at top center.

A PLAN of BOSTON in NEW ENGLAND with its ENVIRONS,
including MILTON, DORCHESTER, ROXBURY, BROOKLIN, CAMBRIDGE, MEDFORD, CHARLESTOWN, Parts of MALDEN and CHELSEA.
With the MILITARY WORKS Constructed in those Places in the Years 1775 and 1776.

view the result was a draw. The Americans were beaten but not shattered. They still had the energy to fortify Winter Hill just beyond Charlestown Neck. The Boston peninsula was still ringed with a chain of fortified hills, any one of which the British might find as costly to take as Breed's Hill. "It is all fortification," Burgoyne wrote. "Driven from one hill, you will see the enemy continually retrenching upon the next; and every step we move must be the slow step of a siege."

On the other hand, Ward's improvised army was incapable of launching an attack on Boston or challenging the British defenses there. As summer gave way to autumn, the two armies did little more than watch each other warily and wait for reinforcements.

At the Battle of Bunker Hill the chief fault on the American side was not cowardice but lack of a proper chain of command. That problem was soon solved. Two days before the battle, the Continental Congress, sitting in Philadelphia, had appointed a Virginia militia colonel, George Washington, "to command all the continental forces, raised or to be raised, for the defense of American liberty." With the arrival of General Washington in Cambridge on July 2, the Massachusetts Provincial army became the Continental army of the thirteen colonies.

There could not have been a more inspired choice than this tall, dignified Virginian. His military experience was large, for he had led expeditions against the French and had served on General Braddock's staff in the ill-fated 1755 campaign against Fort Duquesne. As a southerner he would draw the support of the southern colonies; as an aristocrat he would still the doubts of conservatives fearful of firebrand agitators like Sam Adams; as an experienced military officer he would be able to mold Ward's makeshift force into an army. "I found," Washington wrote of the Cambridge army, "a mixed multitude of People here, under very little discipline, order, or Government . . . Confusion and Disorder reigned . . ."

Washington was not at first discouraged, for he felt that he had the raw material to make into "good Stuff." Order and discipline were the first essentials. The commander-in-chief began by establishing the necessary, if artificial, distinction between officers and enlisted men that Americans have always tended to find irksome in all their wars. Since uniforms were not available—in his blue and buff militia uniform Washington was one of the few properly dressed officers in the whole army—other and simpler distinctions had to be made. A purple ribbon across the chest marked a major general, pink a brigadier, green a staff officer. Majors and colonels wore red or pink cockades in their hats, captains yellow or buff, lieutenants green. Sergeants and corporals fastened red and green shoulder knots on their tunics.

Although he lacked any combat experience, Henry Knox was made commander of the American artillery in late 1775. He became one of Washington's most trusted officers and after the Revolution was appointed the nation's first secretary of war.

Washington's problems were enormous. There was never enough ammunition and powder, those most basic of army commodities. The camp might be temporarily cheered by the arrival of a few companies of frontier riflemen, but the commander-in-chief was faced with the stern prospect of the coming winter. Where would sufficient supplies, equipment, clothing, and food come from? How could his men be sheltered from the northern blizzards? But his immediate problem was manpower. When he took command, he found about 13,000 men fit for duty. Many of them had arrived with heroic ideas about war, ready to fight but scarcely prepared for long and boring months of drill, discipline, and fatigue duties. The realization that any army is first of all a huge housekeeping establishment was too much for many of them.

As the weather turned colder, desertions increased. Ward had persuaded the original volunteers to sign up until the end of 1775 (except for the men from Connecticut, who were engaged only until December 10). When January came, these veterans would be free to go home—and most of them decided that they were going. They felt they had fulfilled their promise, done their share, volunteered their lives, and served their time. Now let somebody else perch uncomfortably on the hills around Boston!

Of the 7,000 men in the eleven old regiments, only 966 could be persuaded to re-enlist for an additional year. At one point Washington was so discouraged that he wrote, "Could I have foreseen what I have, and am likely to experience, no consideration on earth should have induced me to accept this command."

After much cajoling of the newer men, about a quarter of the whole army finally agreed to stay on. Massachusetts and New Hampshire began to raise additional militia units. The Connecticut men were asked to stay until the new soldiers arrived, but they flatly refused. Recruits still continued to trickle in, however, from all over New England.

On New Year's Day, 1776, the new Continental flag was hoisted over the American camp. The crosses of St. George and St. Andrew graced the blue field where the stars are now arranged, but the stripes of red and white for the thirteen colonies were then introduced as we know them in the flag today. In spite of cold, desertions, and reluctant soldiers, Washington gradually managed to build up his army to about 10,000 men—a mixture of veterans, raw recruits, and short-term militia. Those who had left took their muskets with them. But worse than the lack of men in the Continental army was the lack of weapons, above all artillery.

Three hundred roadless miles away at Fort Ticonderoga, artillery was in plentiful supply. This key fortress on Lake Champlain between Canada and British North America had fallen into neglect and half-ruin at the end of

PROSPECT HILL.	BUNKER's HILL.
I. Seven Dollars a Month.	I. Three Pence a Day.
II. Fresh Provisions, and in Plenty.	II. Rotten Salt Pork.
III. Health.	III. The Scurvy.
IV. Freedom, Ease, Affluence and a good Farm.	IV. Slavery, Beggary and Want.

This American propaganda leaflet, contrasting conditions within the British outpost at Bunker Hill and the rebel fort at Prospect Hill on the mainland, was calculated to tempt the redcoats into deserting.

the French Wars. Three weeks after Concord and Lexington, an oddly matched pair—dapper, elegant Benedict Arnold and rough-and-ready Ethan Allen—had led a detachment of eighty-three homespun Vermonters that surprised and captured Ticonderoga's small British garrison. Only one sentry was wounded in this slightly comic engagement. Allen, sword in hand, demanded the fort's surrender from a British officer who had donned his uniform so hastily that he had not had time to put on his breeches. From the ruins of the fort Arnold and Allen secured seventy-eight serviceable cannon, varying from four- to twenty-four-pounders, as well as quantities of cannon balls and powder.

In mid-November, Washington decided to try to bring some of the captured weapons to Boston, even though it meant carting them by ox-drawn sledges down the Hudson Valley and over the steep, snowy barrier of the Berkshires. For this grueling task he picked his twenty-five-year-old artillery officer, Henry Knox.

Knox was a full-faced, florid, good-natured man, an enthusiastic amateur soldier. Tall and stoutly built, he weighed 280 pounds. A few years earlier his London Book-Store, where he sold all the latest books from England, had been an informal intellectual center in Boston. Knox himself read enormously. His hobby was military science, and from military books and his membership in Boston's Ancient and Honourable Artillery Company, he had made himself into a capable artillery officer. He arrived at Ticonderoga to undertake his great task on December 5, 1775.

In the meantime, discouraging as life could be for Washington's Continentals ringing Boston, life within the

John Glover's Marblehead fishermen, known as the "amphibious regiment," march off under the Pine Tree flag to join the Cambridge army in June, 1775. A century and a half later, an old Marblehead resident named John O. J. Frost did this primitive painting. In 1776, Glover's force ferried Washington's men across the ice-choked Delaware to attack Trenton.

In Provincial Congress,

NEW-YORK, August 8th, 1775.

RESOLVED,

THAT the several Committees and Sub-Committees of the different Counties within this Colony, be directed immediately to purchase or hire all the ARMS, with or without Bayonets, that are fit for present Service (on the Credit of this Colony) and to deliver them to the respective Colonels in this Colony employed in the Continental Service, or their Order, for the Use of the CONTINENTAL ARMY.

A true Copy from the Minutes,

ROBERT BENSON, Secry.

The broadside shown here authorized the purchase of muskets, "with or without Bayonets," to arm the ill-equipped Continentals. After Breed's Hill, some Americans were given spears to defend their fortifications.

town was equally bleak for the occupying British. Smallpox raged. The lack of fresh vegetables soon brought scurvy to the reinforced but still demoralized army. Supplies of all kinds, from meat to fuel, had to be shipped from England. The British government sent out massive cargoes to the beleaguered town—5,000 oxen, 14,000 sheep, vast numbers of hogs, 10,000 butts of strong beer, thousands of bushels of coal. Few of these essentials ever arrived. Ships sent from England in the period of autumnal storms foundered or went off course. Animals died at sea. Many a cargo ship was captured by prowling American privateers.

By early autumn Gage's three colleagues agreed that Boston should be abandoned and the bottled-up army evacuated. There was no question of making any more attacks on the Americans when each assault might turn into another Breed's Hill. On October 11, Gage set sail for London, his career in ruins. Howe now commanded all British forces in the thirteen colonies. He would have quit the town at once, but he felt that since he lacked sufficient ships as yet, his troops would have to sit it out until spring.

While the sullen redcoats idly wandered about in Boston's narrow streets, scrounging whatever they could and breaking up wharves, old ships, fences, barns, and sometimes even houses for fuel, the British officers did their makeshift best to amuse themselves. In this they were assisted as much as possible by the local Tories.

Daughters of prominent loyalists took the female parts in plays that the British officers put on in Faneuil Hall, the old "cradle of liberty" which they had made into a theater. Voltaire's *Zara* was produced there during the winter, as well as General Burgoyne's newly written *The Blockade of Boston,* which ridiculed Washington as a country bumpkin. There were sleighing parties, dances, and dinner parties. Pulpit and pews were torn out of the

---

BY HIS EXCELLENCY

WILLIAM HOWE,

MAJOR GENERAL, &c. &c. &c.

AS Linnen and Woolen Goods are Articles much wanted by the Rebels, and would aid and affift them in their Rebellion, the Commander in Chief expects that all good Subjects will ufe their utmoft Endeavors to have all fuch Articles convey'd from this Place: Any who have not Opportunity to convey their Goods under their own Care, may deliver them on Board the Minerva at Hubbard's Wharf, to *Crean Brufh,* Efq; mark'd with their Names, who will give a Certificate of the Delivery, and will oblige himfelf to return them to the Owners, all unavoidable Accidents accepted.

If after this Notice any Perfon fecretes or keeps in his Poffeffion fuch Articles, he will be treated as a Favourer of Rebels.

Bofton, March 10th, 1776.

Howe issued this notice at the beginning of the British evacuation to prevent clothing and blankets from falling into rebel hands.

Henry Knox's men, depicted in a modern painting, struggle to drag their "noble train of artillery" from captured Fort Ticonderoga to Washington's waiting army. Knox thrilled people along the route by occasionally firing "Old Sow," one of his huge mortars.

Old South Meeting House, the floor covered with tanbark, and the building used by the officers as a riding ring, with the gallery serving as a refreshment room.

Other Tories took a more active part in the siege. On the very day of Lexington and Concord several hundred loyalist tradesmen and merchants had offered their services to Gage as gentlemen volunteers. During the summer and autumn such loyalists formed themselves into three volunteer companies: the Loyal American Associators; the Royal Fencible Americans; and—strange as it might seem in the light of Boston's later history—the Loyal Irish Volunteers. The Loyal Americans were commanded by Timothy Ruggles, who had presided over the Stamp Act Congress ten years before and who had the reputation of being one of the best soldiers in the colonies.

Except for minor skirmishes the winter stalemate remained unbroken. In February, Boston harbor froze over, and for a while Washington toyed with the idea of a direct assault on the town until his military council persuaded him to give it up. The situation changed abruptly at the month's end when Knox arrived with the Ticonderoga cannon. He had accomplished a prodigious feat in the bitterest weather, hauling his loads on forty-three sledges he had had constructed and pulled by eighty yoke of oxen. Now he presented his commander with what was indeed "a noble train of artillery"—forty-three cannon, fourteen mortars, and two howitzers.

Washington finally had the long-range weapons to fortify Dorchester Heights. These heights, just across the bay to the southeast of Boston, were as vital to the safety of the town as was Bunker Hill to the north. If Washington could plant his heavy cannon there, he would dominate the town, the fleet, Castle William in the harbor, and the defenses on Boston Neck. Unless Howe could drive the Americans off these heights, he would be forced out of Boston.

Washington made careful and thorough preparations to occupy the heights by surprise before the British caught on to what he was doing. Even with planning and equipment it would be a much more difficult task to accomplish in one night than was Prescott's, since the earth was now frozen to a depth of a foot and a half.

To throw the redcoats off the track, Washington's new artillery began to cannonade Boston from the surrounding hills for three nights beginning on March 2. Extra militiamen were called up, and after dark on March 4 a working party of 1,200 men under John Thomas left Roxbury for Dorchester Heights. Escorting them was a force of eight hundred troops. Hay was piled along the road to screen the 360 oxcarts traveling back and forth with equipment.

With steaming breath and numb fingers, Thomas' men toiled through

The crew from the American ship Franklin *(left) captures a heavily laden British transport near Boston in May of 1776. The English were "intolerably vexed" to learn that they had lost 1,000 carbines and 1,500 barrels of powder in this action.*

the night, setting up heavy timber frames into which they placed previously prepared bundles of sticks called fascines. In front of these fascines they set up barrels filled with earth. There was a bright moon, but enough haze hung over the harbor to conceal the operation from the enemy, and the thunder of the big guns from the farther hills covered up all other sounds. As the picks reached below the frost line the work became easier.

By morning two small redoubts were complete, mounted with cannon, and fully manned—and out of range of British artillery. Only a direct assault could drive out the Continentals now.

At dawn's early light General Howe was astonished and dismayed. "The rebels have done more in one night than my whole army could have done in months," he was heard to remark sourly. Yet the surprise need not have been so complete, for—as at Breed's

Hill—some of the British had become aware during the evening of what was going on. A Lieutenant Colonel Campbell had reported to Colonel Francis Smith at ten o'clock that "the rebels were at work on Dorchester heights." Smith, who seems to have learned little from his experience at Lexington and Concord, characteristically did nothing.

Although Howe had long since determined to quit Boston, his first reaction to Washington's bold stroke was a pugnacious one. He would drive the Continentals from their heights at bayonet point. At once he ordered five regiments of 2,200 regulars to embark from Long Wharf for Castle William. The soldiers carried blankets, a day's supply of food, and canteens filled with rum and water. Their muskets were unloaded—this was to be a matter of cold steel. From Castle William they were to assault the first redoubt while two more regiments, with light infantry and grenadiers, were to attack the second. An American watching the redcoats leave Long Wharf observed that they looked "pale and dejected, and said to one another that it would be another Bunkers-Hill affair or worse."

Fortunately for the gloomy rank and file, Howe's attack plans were interrupted by a howling windstorm—a "Hurrycane," as one Bostonian put it. Then, on the evening of March 5, Howe countermanded his hasty orders. Under the threat of Washington's cannon there was no choice left now for the British but to withdraw.

On March 6 Howe gave orders to evacuate the city, and began his preparations for moving stores and equipment. Days of confusion and plunder followed. What could not be taken was to be destroyed, and some civilians tried hard to turn a profit in the midst of the destruction. Not only were 9,000 soldiers to be transported, but an additional 1,100 Tories, who would not or could not make peace with their opposing countrymen, demanded passage.

Their names included many honored since the early settlement of New England; names like Apthorp, Boylston, Bradstreet, Brattle, Dudley, Faneuil, Hallowell, Lechmere, Pepperrell, Putnam, Quincy, Ruggles, Saltonstall,

The Continental Congress commissioned this medal of George Washington and his officers to commemorate the Boston siege.

MASSACHUSETTS HISTORICAL SOCIETY

EMMET COLLECTION, N.Y. PUBLIC LIBRARY

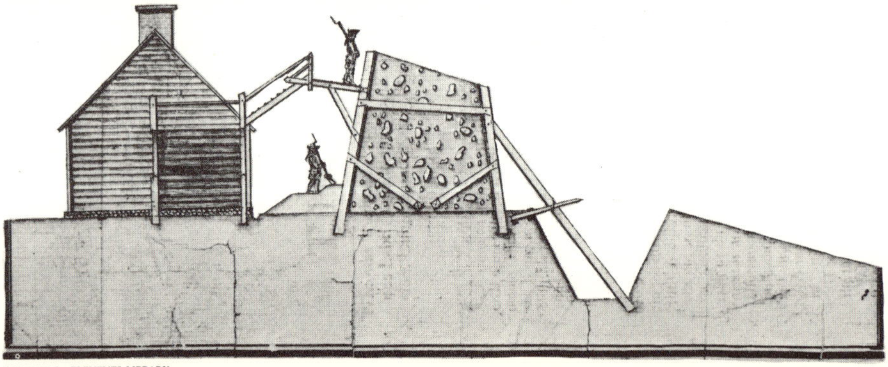

WILLIAM L. CLEMENTS LIBRARY

The contemporary water color above shows British troops surveying the Breed's Hill battlefield. Except for broken fences and the earthen redoubt at right center, little evidence of the bloody fight remained. At left is Captain Montresor's cross-section plan of a part of his powerful fort atop Bunker Hill.

General Howe ordered that all cannon unable to be removed from Boston should be thrown into the harbor. Many of these guns, carelessly spiked, were later recovered and repaired by the Americans. A Tory wrote bitterly that the ships were so jammed that everyone was "obliged to pig together on the floor...."

Sewall, Vassall, Willard, Winslow. But the Tory emigrants were not just the rich and the wellborn. There were many loyalists of modest means, farmers and mechanics, who had endured much for their allegiance to the king and who were now to lose almost everything. Some managed to get a few of their most precious household possessions aboard ship, but at the eleventh hour Howe ordered all furniture and "other useless luggage" to be thrown overboard.

Officially Howe refused to hold any communication with the rebel Washington, but unofficially both sides agreed to a truce. If Howe would withdraw and not burn the town, Washington in turn would hold his fire and do nothing to impede the embarkation of the redcoats.

At nine o'clock on Sunday morning, March 17, 1776—it was St. Patrick's Day—the last of the British garrison and the Tory exiles filed aboard the ships of the fleet. Boston's streets were left strewn with debris and almost deserted. A few redcoats still lingered at Castle William to prepare mines for blowing up the fortifications. During the day they exchanged a few shots with the Americans across the bay, but by evening they too had embarked. As the last British outposts withdrew from the defenses at Boston Neck, a Lieutenant Adair of the marines was sent to scatter crowfeet—sharp four-pointed irons that always landed with one point up—in the no-man's land beyond the gate. "Being an Irishman," one of his fellow officers noted, "he began scattering the crowfeet about from the gate towards the enemy, and of course, had to walk over them on his return, which detained him so long that he was nearly taken prisoner."

Bunker Hill was apparently still manned, but the redcoats in that stronghold seemed suspiciously motionless. Brigadier General John Sullivan and two other American officers, cautiously making their way up the hill, found nothing but dummy sentinels with horseshoes for gorgets and ruffles of paper. One of the scarecrow soldiers had a sign pinned on his chest reading "Welcome Brother Jonathan."

After weighing anchor, the British fleet hove to in Nantasket Roads five miles below Boston, and the sailors spent an additional ten days adjusting the hastily loaded cargoes and taking on water. Finally, on March 27, they put to sea, bound for Halifax, Nova Scotia. From Penn's Hill, Abigail Adams watched the sails billow in the spring breeze. "We have a view of the largest fleet ever seen in America," she wrote. "You may count upwards of a hundred and seventy sail."

And so the history of British rule in Boston ended, with the white sails moving across the blue water like a curtain coming down at the end of a play. The first act had been Lexington and Concord, the climax the Battle of Bunker Hill, and now the last scene faded as the ships dipped one by one below the horizon.

COLLECTION OF GILBERT DARLINGTON

In July, 1776, following a public reading of the Declaration of Independence, New York patriots signaled their defiance of England by toppling the statue of King George III. Afterward, a few enterprising women melted down part of the lead figure for bullets.

AMERICAN HERITAGE PUBLISHING CO., INC.

PRESIDENT JAMES PARTON
EDITORIAL DIRECTOR JOSEPH J. THORNDIKE, JR.
EDITOR, BOOK DIVISION RICHARD M. KETCHUM
ART DIRECTOR IRWIN GLUSKER

AMERICAN HERITAGE JUNIOR LIBRARY

EDITOR STEPHEN W. SEARS
ART DIRECTOR EMMA LANDAU
PICTURE RESEARCHERS JULIA POTTS, *Chief*
  DENNIS A. DINAN · MARY LEVERTY
EDITORIAL ASSISTANT AMY L. RHODES
COPY EDITOR PATRICIA COOPER

ACKNOWLEDGMENTS

The Editors are especially indebted to Mrs. Harriet Ropes Cabot, Curator of Collections at the Bostonian Society in Boston, and to Miss Elizabeth P. Riegel, Supervisor of Sales, Museum of Fine Arts, Boston, for their generous advice and assistance in preparing this book. Thanks are also due the following individuals and institutions:

Albany Institute of History and Art—Janet R. MacFarlane
American Antiquarian Society, Worcester, Mass.—Clifford K. Shipton
Mrs. Anne S. K. Brown, Providence
The John Carter Brown Library, Brown University, Providence—Thomas R. Adams
Mrs. Stedman Buttrick, Sr., Concord, Mass.
Chicago Historical Society—Mrs. Mary Frances Rhymer
Mrs. Maureen Green, London
Massachusetts Historical Society, Boston—Stephen T. Riley, Winifred Collins
National Gallery of Art, Washington—Huntington Cairns
New-York Historical Society—Carolyn Scoon

Photographs of the Doolittle engravings on pages 27 and 31 were furnished through the courtesy of Colonial Williamsburg. The photograph of Revere's Boston Massacre engraving (page 55) was provided by the owner, the Metropolitan Museum of Art, New York; the print is the gift of Mrs. Russell Sage, 1910. The Frick Art Reference Library, New York, supplied the photograph of Clinton on page 79.

FOR FURTHER READING

Alden, John R. *General Gage in America.* Louisiana State University Press, 1948.

The American Heritage Book of the Revolution. American Heritage Publishing Company, 1958.

Bakeless, John. *Turncoats, Traitors and Heroes.* Lippincott, 1959.

Bowen, Catherine Drinker. *John Adams and the American Revolution.* Little, Brown, 1950.

Cary, John. *Joseph Warren—Physician, Politician, Patriot.* University of Illinois Press, 1961.

Clark, William Bell. *George Washington's Navy.* Louisiana State University Press, 1960.

Commager, Henry Steele and Morris, Richard B., editors. *The Spirit of 'Seventy-Six.* Bobbs-Merrill, 1958.

Forbes, Esther. *Paul Revere and the World He Lived In.* Houghton Mifflin, 1942.

French, Allen. *The Day of Concord and Lexington.* Little, Brown, 1936.

French, Allen. *The First Year of the American Revolution.* Houghton Mifflin, 1934.

Frothingham, Richard. *History of the Siege of Boston, and of the Battles of Lexington, Concord, and Bunker Hill.* Little, Brown, 1873.

Gipson, Lawrence H. *The Coming of the Revolution.* Harper's, 1954.

Ketchum, Richard M. *The Battle for Bunker Hill.* Doubleday, 1962.

Lancaster, Bruce. *From Lexington to Liberty.* Doubleday, 1955.

Miller, John C. *Sam Adams, Pioneer in Propaganda.* Little, Brown, 1936.

Murdock, Harold. *The Nineteenth of April, 1775.* Houghton Mifflin, 1925.

Partridge, Bellamy. *Sir Billy Howe.* Longmans, Green & Co., 1932.

Russell, Francis. *The French and Indian Wars.* American Heritage Junior Library, 1962.

Scheer, George F. and Rankin, Hugh F. *Rebels and Redcoats.* World Publishing Company, 1957.

Tourtellot, Arthur B. *William Diamond's Drum.* Doubleday, 1959.

Ward, Christopher. *The War of the Revolution.* Macmillan, 1952.

Index

Bold face indicates pages on which illustrations appear

Abercrombie, Gen., James, 82
Acton, Mass, 23, 28
Adair, Lt., 145
Adams, Abigail, 93, 145
Adams, John, 54, 57, 59
Adams, Samuel, 6, 7, 12, 17, 19, 22, 45, **46,** 48, 49, 52, 54, 57, 59, 62, 65, 66, 70, 73, 130
Adams' Mohawks, 49, 54, 59, 65, *see also* "Loyall Nine," Sons of Liberty
Alexandria, Va., 66
Allen, Ethan, 133
Amherst, Gen. Jeffery, 38, 39, 44

Arlington, *See* Menotomy
Arnold, Benedict, 133
Artillery, British, 32, **76-77,** 91, 93, 98, 103, 107, **144**
  Colonial, 80, 81, 91, 97, **116, 138,** 139
Attucks, Crispus, 54, 56, 57

Baltimore, Md., 66
Barrett, Amos, 23, 30
Barrett, Col. James, 23, 26, 28
Beaver, 62
Bedford, Mass., 23
Bernard, Gov. Francis, 48, 49, 52

150

Bishop, Capt. Thomas, 88
Boston, Mass., **front endsheet,** 11, 12, 14, 16, 17, **16-17** (map), **20-21** (map), 22, 30, 32, 33, **48,** 59, **60-61,** 65, 66, 83, 88, 93, 128, **129** (map), 132, 133, 137, 139, 141, 145
  British occupation of, 52-54, 73-76
  Rioting in, 45-49, 52-57, **55,** 62, **64,** 65, **67**
Boston Common, 12, 17, 52, 53, **53,** 57, 66
Boston Massacre, 7, 54, **55, 56,** 57, 59, 65, 66
Boston Neck, 13, 73, **74-75,** 77, 79, 128, 130, 139, 145
Boston Port Act, 11, 64, 65, 68
Boston Tea Party, 7, 11, 62-65, **64**
Braddock, Gen. Edward, 95, 130
Breed's Hill, **4,** 7, 22, 28, **76-77,** 83, 88-103, **92, 100-101, 104-105** (map), **115, 124-125,** 126, 128, 136, 137, 141, **142-143**
  British assault on, 107-119
  Casualties at, 125, 126
  Topography of, 83
Breed's Hill cyclorama, **102-103, 110-111, 122-123**
Brickett, Lt. Col. James, 81
Bridge, Col. Ebenezer, 81
British government, 11, 33, 38-41, 52, 65, 73, 128, 145, *see also* George III, Parliament
British ships, 83, 86, 91, 92, **104-105** (map), **120-121,** 126, **144,** 145
British troops, 11, 13, **34-35, 53,** 52-54, 70, 73, 79, 80, 91, 95, 98, **102-103, 112-113,** 137
  Grenadiers, 13, 23, **109**
  Light infantry, 13
Brooks, Maj. John, 92
Brown, Peter, 102
Bunker Hill, 76-83, 95, 97, **104-105** (map), 111, 117, 119, 128, 130, 133, 139, 141, 145
  Battle of, 7, 128, 130, 145,
    see also Breed's Hill
  British earthwork on, 76, 77, **76-77,** 83, 128, **142**
  Topography of, 83
Burgoyne, Gen. John, 73, 74, **78,** 87, 90, 123, 125, 130, 137
Buttrick, Maj. John, 22, 28, 35

Caldwell, James, 54, 56, 57
Cambridge, 13, 14, **16-17** (map), 19, 33, 72, 73, 77, 79, 81, 98, **129** (map), 130

Campbell, Lt. Col., 144
Carr, Patrick, 54, 56, 57, 59
Castle William, **48,** 49, 52, 57, 62, 139, 141, 145
Cerberus, 73
Chappel, Alonzo, paintings by, **34-35, 124-125**
Charles River, 11, 13, 14, **16-17** (map), 83, 87, 88, 90, 102, 114
Charleston, S.C., 59, 62, 66
Charlestown, Mass., 12, 13, 14, **16-17** (map), 65, **74-75,** 76, 80, 83, 88, 98, **100-101,** 102, **104-105** (map), 107, 110, **116, 120-121, 122-123,** 125, 126
Charlestown Neck, 33, 83, 88, 126, 130
Clark, Rev. Jonas, 14, 17
Clinton, Gen. Henry, 73, 77, **79,** 87, 90, 105, 114, 116, 117, 123, 125, 128
Colden, Gov. Cadwallader, 42
Colonial army, *See* Continental army, Minutemen, Provincial army
Committee of Correspondence, 59, 65
Committee of Safety, 32, 70, 79, 92
Conant, Col. William, 12
Concord, Mass., 7, 12, 13, 14, 16, **16-17** (map), 19, **20-21** (map), 22, 23, **23,** **24-25,** 26, **27,** 28, 30, 33, 34, 70, 128
Connecticut, 81, 97, 102
Continental army, 73, 130, 132, 133, 141
Continental Congress, First, 12, 66
Continental Congress, Second, 12, 70, 73, 130, 141
Continental flag, 132
Copley, John Singleton, 7, paintings by, **10, 46, 47, 71, 94**
Copp's Hill battery, Boston, 76, 77, **76-77,** 83, 91, **104-105** (map), 107, **120-121**

Dartmouth, 62
Davis, Isaac, 28
Dawes, William, 13-16, **15**
Diamond, William, 19
Doolittle, Amos, engravings by, **18, 27, 31**
Dorchester Heights, **16-17** (map), 76, 77, 79, 128, **129** (map), 139, 141

Earle, Ralph, 18, painting by, **24-25**
East India Company, 11, 59
Eleanor, 62

151

Emerson, Ralph Waldo, quoted, 21

Falcon, 86
Faneuil Hall, Boston, 38, 62, 137
Fawkes, Guy, 45
Fort Ticonderoga, N.Y., 34, 132, 133, 138, 139
Franklin, **140**
Franklin, Benjamin, 33, 34
French and Indian Wars, 19, 34, 38, 39, 73, 82, 95, 98, 118, 126, 130, 132
Frost, John O. J., painting by, **134-135**
Frye, Col. James, 81

Gage, Gen. Thomas, 12, 13, 19, 28, 30, 52, 65, 66, 72-77, 87, 88, 90, **94,** 97, 126, 128, 137, 139
Gainsborough, Thomas, painting by, **29**
Gaspee, **58**
George II, King of England, 39
George III, King of England, 12, 35, 39, 40, 48
    Coat of arms of, **38**
    Statue of, **146-147**
Glasgow, 86, **100-101,** 125
Glover, John, 135
Gordon Riots, 44
Graves, Adm. Samuel, 76, 88, 98
Gray, Samuel, 54, 56, 57, 83
Great Britain, *See* British government
Greene, Gen. Nathanael, 79
Grenville, George, 40-42, **43**
Gridley, Col. Richard, 81, 83, 87
Gridley, Capt. Samuel, 81, 91, 92, 97, 117
Griffin's Wharf, Boston, 62, 65
Guy Fawkes Day, 45

Hancock, John, 6, 7, 12, 17, **47,** 51, 65, 66, 70
Harvard College, 72, 81, **84-85**
Henry, Patrick, quoted, 7
Hosmer, Joseph, 26
Howe, Lord George Augustus, 34
Howe, Gen. William, 73, 87, 88, 90, 95, 98, 103-107, **106,** 109, 110, 114, 117, 123, 128, 137, 140, 141, 144, 145
Hubbard, Ebenezer, 23
Hutchinson, Gov. Thomas, 42, 48, 49, 57, 62, 65

King Street, Boston, 49, 52, 54, 57
Knowlton, Capt. Thomas, 83, **96,** 97, 102, 111, 123
Knox, Henry, **131,** 133, 138, 139

Langdon, Rev. Dr. Samuel, 81
Larkin, Deacon John, 13
Laurie, Capt. Walter, 26-28
Lexington, Mass., 7, 12-14, 16, **16-17** (map), **18,** 19, **20-21** (map), 22, 23, 28, 30-34, **31, 34-35,** 70, 128, 133, 139, 145
Liberty, 51
Liberty Tree, the, 42, 50, 56, **68**
Lively, 86, 88
Long Wharf, Boston, **front endsheet, 50-51,** 52, 74, **74-75,** 91, 126, 141
Louisbourg, siege of, 19, 34, 73, 80, 81, 98
Loyalists, 39, 137, 139, *see also* Tories
"Loyall Nine," 48, 49, 54, *see also* Adams' Mohawks, Sons of Liberty

McClary, Andrew, **96**
Marblehead regiment, **134-135**
Massachusetts, 81, 102, 132
Maverick, Samuel, 56, 57
Medford, Mass., 14, 83
Menotomy (Arlington), Mass., 13, 14, **16-17** (map), 32, 33
Meriam's Corner, Mass., 30
Minutemen, 12-35, 70, 72, *see also* Provincial army
Mob action, 7, 41-45, 48, 49, 52-57, 65, *see also* Boston Massacre, Boston Tea Party
Montresor, Capt. John, 76, 83, 128, 143
Morton's Hill, 83, 97, 107
Morton's Point, 93, 95, 98, 126
Munroe, Robert, 19, 22
Mystic River, 14, **16-17** (map), 83, 88, 90, 95, 97, 102

New Hampshire, 40, 93, 102, 132
New York, 12, 41, 59, 62
Newman, Robert, 13
North, Lord Frederick, 65, **68**
North Battery Wharf, Boston, 91
North Bridge, Concord, 14, **16-17** (map), **20-21** (map), 23, 26, **27,** 28, 34

152

North Church, Boston, 12, 13, **74-75**
Nutting, Capt. John, 83, 87

Old South Meeting House, Boston, 54, 65, 66, 139
Old State House, Boston, 49, 54, **55, 60-61,** 65
Oliver, Andrew, 42, 48

Parker, Capt. John, 19, 21, 22, 30
Parliament, British, 11, 39, **40,** 41, 45, 50, 59, 65
Parsons, Capt., 23, 26, 28, 30
Peale, Charles Willson, painting by, **82**
   Sketch by, **116**
Pelham, Henry, map by, **129**
Percy, Hugh, Earl, **28,** 31, 32, 33, 35, 66
Philadelphia, 12, 59, 62, 66
Pigot, Gen. Robert, 98, 102, 105, 110, 114, 117, 119
Pine Tree flag, **96**
Pitcairn, Maj. John, 13, **18,** 19, 21, **22,** 23, **24-25,** 105, 119, 123
Pollard, Asa, 90
Pomeroy, Gen. Seth, 98, 122
Pope's Day, 44, 45
Pope's carriage, **44,** 45
Prescott, Dr. Samuel, 16
Prescott, Col. William, 79, 80, 81, 83, 86-88, 90-92, **96,** 97, 98, 102, 108, 111, 114, 117, 119, 128
Preston, Capt. John, 56, 57, 59
Propaganda & satire, British, **43, 52, 66, 68,** 137
   Colonial, **36-37,** 54, 57, 59, **63,** 70, **72,** 133, 136
Province House, Boston, 74, 87, 90, 91, 128
Provincial army, 72, 73, 79, 81, **88, 89,** 97, 98, 102-125, 130, *see also* Continental army, Minutemen
Provincial Congress, 66, 70, 81, 98
Putnam, Gen., Israel, 72, 79, 81, 83, 92, 97, 98, 111, 117, **118**
Pyle, Howard, painting by, **112-113**

Quincy, Dolly, 66
Quincy, Josiah, 57, 59, 65

Ramsay, Allan, painting by, **78**

Ranney, William T., painting by, **6**
Reed, James, 93, 95, 102
Remick, Christian, 52, painting by, **50-51**
Revere, Paul, 7, **10,** 11-17, 32
   Engravings by, **front endsheet, 55, 56, 84-85**
Rhode Island, 58, 79
Rockingham, Lord Charles, 42, 49
Royal Marines, 12, 13, **122-123**
Royal Navy, 73, 95, 98, 107
Royal Welch Fusiliers, 11, 108, 109
Roxbury, Mass., **16-17** (map), 73, 76, 77, 80, 139

Smith, Col. Francis, 13, 17, 19, 22, 23, **24-25,** 26, 28, 30-33, 81, 141
Somerset, 11, 76
Sons of Liberty, 39, 41, 42, 48, 49, 52, 53, 57, 59, 62, 66, *see also* Adams' Mohawks, "Loyall Nine"
Stamp Act, 40-43, 48-50
Stamp Act Congress, 41, 139
Stark, Gen. John, 93, 95, 97, 98, 103, 108, 122, 123
Stuart, Gilbert, 7, paintings by, **127, 131**
Symmetry, 86, **100-101**

Tea Act, 59, 62, 63
Thomas, Gen., John, 79, 139
Tories, 66, 73, 74, 139, 141, 145, *see also* Loyalists
Townshend, Charles, 50
Townshend Acts, 50, 59
Trevett, Capt. Samuel, 97, 125
Trumbull, John, painting by, **96, back endsheet**
   Sketches by, **118, 119**

Ward, Gen. Artemas, 72, 73, 79, 80, **82,** 92, 128, 130, 132
Warren, Dr. Joseph, 12, 33, 34, 70-73, **71,** 92, 98, 122, **back endsheet**
Washington, Gen., George, **127,** 130-133, 137-139, 141, 145
Whigs, 12, 57, 66, 70, 73, 81
Willard, Abijah, 93
Willard, Archibald, painting by, **cover**
Wolfe, Gen. James, 34, 73, 81
Wright's Tavern, Concord, 23, 26